Eyewitness
WILD WEST

Mexican soldier

Ghost shirt

Cowboy boots

Stetson

Miner's pickaxe

Pan for washing gold

Compass of Lewis and Clark

Daniel Boone's rifle

Eyewitness
WILD WEST

Written by
STUART MURRAY

Sheriff's badge

Prarie schooner

THE GREAT TRAIN ROBBERY
WRITTEN BY SCOTT MARBLE

WRESTLING FOR WEALTH.
A DARE-DEVIL COW-BOY TRIUMPHS OVER AN ENORMOUS GRIZZLY.

Theater poster

DK

In Association with the
Smithsonian Institution

Trapper's otterskin hat

LONDON, NEW YORK, MUNICH,
MELBOURNE, and DELHI

MEDIA PROJECTS INC.
Executive Editor C. Carter Smith
Managing Editor Carter Smith
Project Editor Aaron Murray
Designer Laura Smyth
Design Consultants Sherry Williams, Tilman Reitzle
Photo Researcher Athena Angelos

DK PUBLISHING
Editor Beth Sutinis
Senior Art Editor Michelle Baxter
Art Director Tina Vaughan
Jacket Art Director Dirk Kaufman
Publisher Andrew Berkhut
Production Manager Chris Avgherinos

REVISED EDITION
Editors Elizabeth Hester, Carter Smith
Publishing director Beth Sutinis
Art director Dirk Kaufman
DTP designer Milos Orlovic
Production Chris Avgherinos, Ivor Parker

This edition published in the United States in 2005
by DK Publishing, Inc.
375 Hudson Street, New York, NY 10014

05 06 07 08 09 10 9 8 7 6 5 4 3 2 1

Library of Congress Cataloging-in-Publication Data
Murray, Stuart, 1948-
Wild West / by Stuart Murray.
p. cm. — (Eyewitness books)
Summary: Brief text and color illustrations chronicle the
history of the American West, from the adventures of Lewis and Clark
to the massacre at Wounded Knee.
ISBN 0-7566-1097-4 (hc) — ISBN 0-7566-1098-2 (lib. bdg.)
1. West (U.S.)—History—To 1848—Juvenile literature.
2. West (U.S.)—History—1848-1860—Juvenile literature. 3. West
(U.S.)—History—1860-1890—Juvenile literature. [1. West (U.S.)—
History.] I. Title. II. DK eyewitness books.
F591 .M936 2001
978'.02—dc21

2001028156

Color reproduction by
Colourscan, Singapore
Printed in China by Toppan Printing Co.,
(Shenzhen) Ltd.

Discover more at
www.dk.com

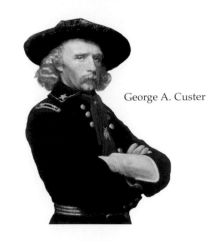

George A. Custer

Six-shooter

Railroad poster

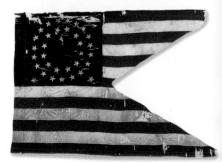

Cavalry pennant

Totem pole

Beaver

Contents

Steam locomotive

The Western wilderness

THE WEST BEGINS AT THE GREAT PLAINS, which stretch 500 miles to the Rocky Mountains. Many biological communities are found here, including tundra, prairie, desert, and forest. The Pacific coast has giant trees, while the central grasslands have only small groves of cottonwood. In deserts, where little else grows, sagebrush and cactus thrive, sheltering a variety of creatures. The eagle, coyote, rattlesnake, jackrabbit, and prairie dog are found almost everywhere. The wolf once was common, as were bobcat and mountain lion. Bighorn sheep, moose, caribou, grizzly bear, and deer shared the high country. Elk and antelope roamed the grasslands, where herds of bison (buffalo) once numbered 75 million. By 1900, overhunting had reduced the bison to about 1,000.

THE COYOTE'S CRY
The yipping of coyotes is heard throughout the West as the sun goes down. The coyote hunts rodents and hares and sometimes domestic animals, but avoids humans.

The Great Plains

"The Great American Desert" was the name explorers gave to the semi-arid region that stretches from the Missouri River to the Rocky Mountains. At first, this treeless land, with little rainfall, few rivers or streams, and long, hot summers, was described as a wasteland. Yet, livestock found rich grass here, and grain crops thrived, especially wheat. Windmills pumped water to the surface, and soil and water conservation, along with irrigation, turned the Great Plains into a world leader in wheat and beef production.

PRAIRIE DOGS
Prairie dogs once were abundant in the American West. Their colonies on the plains had hundreds of funnel-shaped mounds indicating entrances to burrows. Farmers and herders have tried to get rid of prairie dogs, claiming they compete with cattle for grasslands and destroy crops.

Buffalo were hunted for their hides

Horns used to make cups, fire carriers, and ladles by native peoples

Two-toed feet with hooves

Long, woolly hair makes bison appear larger to predators

THE BUFFALO
Bison – or buffalo – once moved in vast, grazing herds, like shadows on the plains. One of the most formidable American animals, the buffalo bull can weigh 2,000 pounds. Native peoples always had hunted buffalo as an important source of food and household products, but spreading settlement and professional hide hunters soon destroyed the herds.

Rugged mountains and harsh deserts

The western landscape can seem ideal for vegetation and wildlife – or completely unlivable. Yet, there are plants and animals thriving everywhere. The West includes the Central Lowlands of the easterly regions, with broad rivers and muddy bottomlands. Farther west rise semi-arid grasslands called the Great Plains. High-peaked mountain ranges march thousands of miles from Canada to Mexico and along the Pacific Coast. Pine forests and mountain meadows of High Plateau country border great deserts and flat, arid basins. In each region there are distinctive flora and fauna, perfectly adapted for survival.

THE EAGLE
Pioneers found birds in abundance in the West, with the eagle as lord of them all. Eagles range over mountain and prairie, ready to dive for prairie dogs or jackrabbits or snatch up fish in shallow pools.

Talons for grasping prey

MOUNTAIN PANORAMA
The Cascades of Washington State are in the Northern Rocky Mountain Range – part of a chain of peaks stretching southward to New Mexico. Fed by snow and rain, many western rivers rise in the Rockies, including the Colorado, North Platte, South Platte, Snake, Arkansas, and Rio Grande.

Rattle

A RATTLER
The West is home to many poisonous rattlesnakes. The diamond-back is the largest of 30 species. When in danger, the dry skin at the end of their tails rattles with a buzzing noise to warn that the snake is ready to strike.

THE BOBCAT
This wide-ranging cat with the "bobbed," or short, tail has long legs and large paws and is an effective predator. Solitary and nocturnal (ranging at night and sleeping by day), the bobcat eats rodents, rabbits, hares, and birds.

THE LONG-LIVED SAGUARO
This tall cactus, with arms like columns, can live for 200 years. The saguaro (pronounced su-WA-ro) is the symbol of Arizona, which has adopted its white blossom as the state flower. Because of their long, straight branches, reaching as high as 16 feet, saguaros are sometimes called the organ-pipe cactus. They are found in the Sonoran Desert, which extends from the Gulf of California northeastward to Arizona and northwestward to Southern California.

CANYON COUNTRY
Over millions of years, the Colorado River Plateau's high desert country has been slashed and cut by the erosion of wind and water. The resulting canyon lands have spectacular gorges worn as deep as 5,000 feet below the surface. The greatest is Arizona's 217 mile-long Grand Canyon.

The spirit of Native America

THE LAND AND ALL ITS CREATURES were treated with respect by the original nations of the American West. Animals were hunted to provide the food, clothing, and shelter that were the principle support of Indian life. Rituals of many kinds were believed to help maintain good relations between the people and the natural world. For example, pictures of buffalo or elk were placed on Indian weapons to aid in the hunt, and eagle feathers were worn by warriors as a sign of power. Native peoples believed certain rituals were necessary to prepare them for communication with the spirit world.

SACRED SYMBOLS
The peoples of the Northwest coast, such as the Tsimshian and Haida, carved images of animals and mythical creatures onto poles that might support a house roof or mark a grave. Known as totems, these images belonged to the family that had them carved.

The Thunderbird with feathers and curved beak

A totem pole for a grave site

PROTECTION IN WAR
This head chief of the Blackfoot, a mighty nation of the Great Plains, was in full war regalia when he sat for a portrait in 1832. His deerskin tunic is decorated with an embroidered medallion.

Eagle feather

Locks of hair taken from enemies killed in battle

Design made of dyed porcupine quills

FUNERAL ON THE PLAINS
A Crow woman mourns her husband, whose body lies on a platform hung with the heads of his favorite ponies. They were expected to accompany him in the next world.

Five-foot-long ceremonial pipe

Apache crown dancers

Symbol depicts the buffalo

AN APACHE CHRONICLE
Using pictographs – images that tell stories – an artist of the Southwest's Apache tribe illustrated their "Crown Dance" on this antelope skin. Wearing brightly colored wooden head dresses, the Apache dancers called upon the *gans*, or nature spirits, to guide their people and cure illness.

Painted antelope skin

Hair of the White Buffalo, a young rainmaker

BUFFALO SHIELD
The feathers of the eagle, a symbol of power and speed, decorate this Pawnee shield made of buffalo hide. The shield bears the head of a buffalo bull, honoring this mightiest creature of the Great Plains. Buffaloes provided essential food, clothing, and shelter for many Indian nations.

Eagle feathers

MAKING RAIN
In a painting done from life in the early 19th century, a Mandan youth stands on the roof of a lodge near the Missouri River and calls for nature to send much-needed rain. The custom of the Mandans was for young men to take turns dancing and singing until it rained, or until they were too weary to go on. This rainmaker was successful, for when he shot an arrow into a black cloud hanging overhead, rain began to fall in torrents.

PURIFYING SMOKE
In the late 1880s, an artist depicted these Blackfoot men of southeastern Montana burning Sweetgrass. They believed the smoke would ritually cleanse them. The men are preparing medicine bags – collections of charms – which include bones, beads, herbs, feathers, good-luck tokens, and animal or human hair. These charms will be purified by the smoke.

Daily life in Native America

THE ORIGINAL PEOPLES OF THE EARLY 19TH-CENTURY West were as different from each other as the vast lands they lived upon. Some Indian men were expert riders who could lean over the neck of a galloping pony and fire an arrow accurately, but many more were farmers, artisans, and fishermen. Mounted warriors of the central plains frequently raided their neighbors, but the peaceable communities of the Southwest were best known for hand crafts such as pottery, weaving, and jewelry. The nomadic nations followed buffalo herds and made temporary homes in hide tepees, while the folk of the northwest coast had wooden houses and built longboats for whale-hunting. Still other nations were successful traders and travelers in regular contact with white civilization. Yet, no matter where or how western Native Americans lived in this time, their lives soon would be changed forever by a sudden and unwanted flood of outsiders into their land.

Supporting poles

Smoke opening

Entrance

A TOY TEPEE
Crafted for a Lakota Sioux child, this miniature tepee copies the full-size structure. Hides are laid over long poles that meet at the top. Smoke from the tepee's central fire rises through an opening that can be changed in size by moving the flaps.

People of the Plains

The nations of the Great Plains, such as the Sioux, Comanche, and Crow, followed migrating herds of bison – or buffalo – which they hunted. These Indians were masterful riders, who bred quick, strong ponies for hunting and battle. When a family decided to move, its tepee was taken down and folded up for transport to the next campsite. In just a few hours, the tepee would be erected again. Tepees varied in size, with the largest being 25 feet in diameter, requiring 14 stitched bison skins to cover its supporting poles.

Decorative design

SADDLE FOR A SIOUX
The excellent horsemanship of the Plains Indians made the rider and mount seem like one. Indeed, there was little gear between the horse and rider, as shown by this Sioux warrior's light saddle with its slender straps. Many Indians rode bareback, but for long journeys, a hide saddle stuffed with buffalo or deer hair was more comfortable.

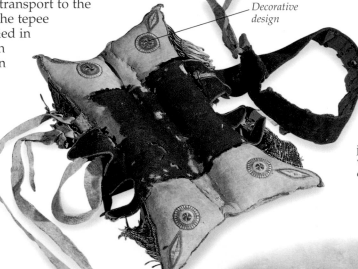

Saddle strap

MOTHER AND CHILD
During his travels through the West, painter George Catlin depicted this young Plains Indian woman, named Chee-Ah-Ka-Tchee, and her baby, who is wrapped closely in a colorful quilled cradle.

THE FATAL BLOW
Hunting fleeing buffalo from the back of a galloping horse demanded great skill and courage, as shown in this painting of riders in pursuit of a herd. A warrior races close alongside the buffalo, preparing to throw his spear into the animal's side.

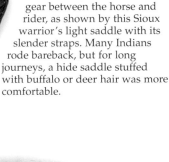

COMING FOR THE BRIDE
The honored groom is carried by canoe to meet his bride for a wedding ceremony of the Kwakiutl tribe in the Pacific Northwest. The figure in the bow of the canoe is dressed as a Thunderbird, bringing good fortune to the newlyweds.

Ceremonial Thunderbird costume

A CHILD'S DRESS
Some fortunate child of the Crow tribe wore this dress, which must have been a labor of love. The dress was carefully decorated with elk teeth, probably by a woman member of the child's family, perhaps a grandmother or an older sister. The Crow people lived between the eastern Rockies and the Missouri River.

Elk tooth decoration

A SUN-BAKED PUEBLO
The Hopi inhabitants of this Arizona village live on various levels that are reached by long ladders. This pueblo, as a village of sun-dried mud brick is known, was surrounded by farmlands. Named Walpi, this pueblo is on the site of a village that existed long before Europeans arrived in the 1500s, making it one of the oldest continuously inhabited places in North America.

The explorers

THE U.S. GOVERNMENT PURCHASED a vast western region, called Louisiana, from France in 1803, and a year later sent explorers to make maps of the land and learn what was there. Led by Meriwether Lewis and William Clark, the expedition journeyed for two years, reaching the Pacific coast. Their interpreter was Sacajawea, a Shoshoni woman, who assured the native peoples the explorers were friendly. Many more western expeditions went out in the next 90 years, seeking the source of rivers, crossing the desert Southwest, and investigating unknown mountain ranges. The expeditions included mapmakers, surveyors, scientists, artists, and photographers. As head of the newly established U.S. Geological Survey from 1881–1884, John Wesley Powell promoted scientific study of the West, especially of the region's precious water resources.

THE WAY WEST
The Lewis and Clark expedition followed the Missouri River westward to its headwaters, crossed the Rocky Mountains, then journeyed to where the Columbia River flows into the Pacific Ocean.

Lewis

Clark

Lewis and Clark

President Thomas Jefferson sent the Lewis and Clark Corps of Discovery on an 8,000-mile journey into the unknown western wilderness. This expedition strengthened American claims to much of the trans-Mississippi West – the lands beyond the Mississippi River.

Compass of Lewis and Clark

PEACE MEDALS
President Jefferson's image and the slogan "Peace and Friendship" decorate this 1801 silver and copper medal Lewis and Clark gave to native peoples to win their trust.

FIERCE BUT FRIENDLY
On the Columbia River late in 1805, Indians in war canoes and battle regalia meet the Lewis and Clark expedition for the first time. Translator Sacajawea gestures with sign language to an approaching canoe.

FREMONT'S TRIUMPH
A postage stamp was issued in 1842 to honor John Frémont's expedition that explored and surveyed the Rocky Mountains. A few years later, from 1846–1847, Frémont led a troop of volunteers in the struggle to take California from Mexico.

CLIFFS OF THE UPPER COLORADO
While traveling with a geological expedition in 1871, artist Thomas Moran (1837–1926) experienced the intense colors the reflected sun produced on the bluffs of the upper Colorado River in Wyoming Territory. Moran's artwork helped convince the government to set aside large portions of the West as national parks.

Camera lens could be turned to focus

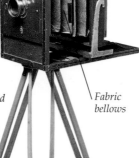

Tripod legs fold to transport camera easily

Fabric bellows

A RISKY PERCH
A daring photographer sets his camera atop Glacier Point to photograph Yosemite Falls in California, during an 1880s surveying expedition. Photographers often tried for the most dramatic shot they could get.

SURVEYOR'S CAMERA
This bulky camera and tripod, weighing as much as 70 pounds, were carried on the 1872 Powell journey through the Colorado River's Grand Canyon.

SCIENTIST AND LINGUIST
Explorer, surveyor, and naturalist John Wesley Powell (1834–1902), who studied languages of the native peoples, speaks with Paiute chief Tau-Gu. The Paiutes are a tribe of the Great Basin, which includes Nevada and western Utah and parts of California and Oregon. Man-made Lake Powell, in this region, was named in the scientist's honor.

Eyepiece *Adjustment* *Front lens*

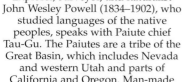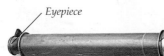

Explorer's telescope

Across the Appalachians

WARRIOR'S PATH
Native travelers moved swiftly over ancient hunting trails and war paths, such as this one in the Allegheny Mountains. Forest trails joined distant Indian villages with the settled white farmlands of the East and South.

LATE IN THE 1700S, the forests and rushing rivers beyond the Appalachian Mountains called to thousands of Americans who felt it was too crowded in the East and Southeast. Most were farmers who wanted to settle in rich new lands, where no whites yet lived. Led by experienced hunters such as Daniel Boone, hundreds of families began to make their way over the Appalachians, seeking the country known as Kentucky. To get there, pioneers cut the Wilderness Road, which wound through the Cumberland Gap, a narrow opening in the mountains. This trickle of westward migration soon became a flood. Between 1775 and 1800, more than 300,000 pioneers crossed into Kentucky. There they erected strong forts and blockhouses to defend against attacks by native peoples who were angry at being pushed aside by the newcomers. Settlers built sturdy log cabins with musket loopholes and stout doors for protection against Indian raids. In time, their settlements in Kentucky and neighboring Tennessee, became starting points for the next wave of westward migration.

INTO THE WILDERNESS
Daniel Boone (1734–1820) leads pioneers through the Cumberland Gap in 1773, heading for Kentucky. Cherokees attacked and drove Boone's party back. Two years later, he and the settlers came again, this time to stay.

RAISING A CABIN
Friends and neighbors on the frontier joined together to help build homes that also served as small forts. The snug and sturdy log cabin, made of spruce or pine logs, was the most common home for pioneers who crossed the Appalachians.

Watch tower

FORT BOONESBOROUGH
Boone's first settlement, with ten-foot-high walls, was built near the Kentucky River in 1775 on land the settlers bought from a Cherokee chief. Not all the tribes recognized the sale, however, and Boonesborough was often in danger from other Cherokees and from Shawnees.

THE LONG RIFLE
White hunters carried rifles such as this one, which belonged to Daniel Boone. With 46-inch barrels, they were called long rifles and were extremely accurate. The best were made in Pennsylvania, but named Kentucky rifles because pioneers there favored them.

Boone's initials

Long barrel

Ceremonial paint

A SHAWNEE WARRIOR
No nation fought harder against white settlement than the Shawnee of the upper Ohio River, who were not defeated until 1825. This portrait of the Shawnee named Payta Kootha illustrates how the warrior decorated his face with bright paint, while favoring the finest style of clothing.

Looped earrings

SHAWNEE BOW AND ARROWS
After 1750, native hunters and warriors used bows and arrows only when they could not get firearms and ammunition. Although most Indians were independent, they needed trade with whites.

WAR AND PESTILENCE!
Readers were sure to buy newspapers telling the latest sensational stories of Indian attacks and plagues. Dreaded news of cholera striking the cities and of Indian attacks on frontier settlements sent a shudder through eastern communities, where newspapers sold the best.

War and Pestilence!

HORRIBLE AND UNPARALELLED MASSACRE!

Women and Children
FALLING VICTIMS TO THE
INDIAN'S TOMAHAWK.

While many of our most populous cities have been visited by that dreadful disease, the Cholera, and to which thousands have fallen victims, the merciless Savages have been as fatally engaged in the work of death on the frontiers ; where great numbers (including women and children) have fallen victims to the bloody tomahawk.

THE LEGENDARY BOONE
Images of frontier wars usually showed whites as heroes and Indians as villains. In fact, both peoples committed deeds of heroism and cruelty. Daniel Boone, pictured saving a woman and child from a threatening warrior, was the most famous frontier hero of the late 1700s.

Fort Dearborn's wall

A QUILTED FORTRESS
Patchwork was a favorite pastime of frontier women, who created this "Great Quilt" in the early 1800s. It shows the layout of Fort Dearborn on the shore of Lake Michigan. The scene of a massacre of whites and their Indian allies during the War of 1812, Fort Dearborn eventually became the city of Chicago.

Pushing westward

THE SOUTH'S "FIVE CIVILIZED TRIBES" – Cherokee, Seminole, Choctaw, Creek, and Chickasaw – owned well-built houses in villages with mission schools. The Cherokee even published a newspaper using their own alphabet, invented by Sequoyah, their greatest scholar. These peoples wanted peace, but land-hungry whites invaded their country, and war erupted. One of the worst battles was in 1813 at Horseshoe Bend, Alabama, where General Andrew Jackson's army killed more than 800 Creek men, women, and children. The Cherokee nation appealed to the courts to be left alone. While the Supreme Court supported them, the state governments, Congress, and President Andrew Jackson did not. The government's Indian Removal Act of 1830 forced most of these tribes into the new Indian Territory beyond the Mississippi. Many died journeying there on the route named The Trail of Tears. Florida's Seminole, led by Chief Osceola, fought the longest Indian war of all, lasting until 1847.

FEATHERED BEAUTY
This dance wand, decorated with plumes of feathers, was used in traditional ceremonies by the Cherokees.

CHEROKEE SCHOLAR
Sequoyah (ca.1770–1843) was a Cherokee silversmith who migrated with his people to Indian Territory in 1818. There, he developed a written Cherokee language with 86 characters – a syllabary – matching the sounds of the spoken word. A Cherokee printing press was created in 1828, on which the *Cherokee Phoenix* newspaper was printed.

Onto the Reservation

The policy of moving native peoples from their homelands required new land grants to be opened – reserved – for them. In the 1820s, a reservation, called Indian Territory, was being established west of the Mississippi. By 1885, some 50 tribes had been moved to the region known as Oklahoma, a Choctaw term meaning red people.

Sioux

Chippewa and Ottawa

Sauk and Fox

Miami

Wyandot

Shawnee

Indian Territory

Trail of Tears

Chickasaw   Cherokee

Choctaw

Creek

Seminole

TRAIL OF TEARS
Forced to move westward, the Cherokees were escorted by soldiers on a hard and sorrowful journey they called The Trail of Tears. Of 15,000 Cherokees who left their homeland, as many as 4,000 died on the way. It was the same with other tribes; from a group of 1,000 Choctaws, only 88 survived the trek.

Seminole Wars

The Seminole people of Florida lived alongside former black slaves who had run away from plantations. When the government ordered the Seminoles to move onto a reservation, they resisted fiercely, fighting two wars between 1816–1847. At last outnumbered, many Seminoles fled deep into the swamp lands, refusing to be relocated.

OSCEOLA (1804–1837)
For twenty years, Chief Osceola fought for the Seminoles and was their greatest leader. Tricked by a flag of truce, he was captured in 1837 and soon died. Osceola's people continued to fight for 10 more years.

Ostrich plumes

Silver crescents hang from neck

Buttoned leggings

INVASION AND MASSACRE
After American troops invaded Florida in 1817, brutal wars raged for more than 30 years. There were victories and defeats on both sides, including this slaughter of white settlers.

BATTLE AT LAKE OKEECHOBEE
Most fighting during the Seminole Wars involved hit-and-run attacks and ambushes, but an 1837 clash along Lake Okeechobee's shores pitted 1,000 soldiers against 500 Seminoles. Commanded by future president Colonel Zachary Taylor, the army defeated the outnumbered natives near the military blockhouse in this painting.

Patchwork patterns

Large sleeves

SEMINOLE DESIGN
Traditional Seminole dolls made of palmetto fiber were handcrafted long before whites arrived in America and were often used for trading. This doll is dressed in a man's smock known as a big shirt. These smocks were decorated with colorful patchwork and fit loosely with wide sleeves, to help the wearer stay cool.

EVERGLADES HOME
Offering shade in the heat of the Florida summer and able to shed heavy rains, the Seminole house was open-walled with an interior platform and a thatched roof. Known as *chikees*, these houses were usually occupied by one family. Chickees without a platform were built around a communal fire. Chikees were well suited as shelters in the steamy Everglades swamp lands, where many Seminoles still live today.

Trappers and mountain men

The "fast young men," some called them, and the mountain trappers of the 1840s and 1850s lived up to that name. Placing traps for beaver in icy streams, living as equals with the Indian community, these most rugged of individuals knew no master but themselves. They faced death from fierce weather or fiercer native enemies, from their own kind during a drunken brawl, or in encounters with grizzly bears. Their greatest joy was at summer rendezvous, where they sold their beaver pelts, raced horses, wrestled, drank, and danced the night away. The most famous mountain men – Jim Bridger, Jim Beckwourth, and Jedediah Smith – were the West's best scouts and guides. They led the way for soldiers, missionaries, and wagon trains to follow. And as civilization took over, the mountain men melted away, like the independent tribes, the beaver, and the wild game that had sustained their free and colorful way of life.

ON WESTERN WATERS
From 1658 to 1671, explorer Pierre Radisson (1636–1710) searched for a waterway to the Pacific Ocean. Leading expeditions into Wisconsin and the upper Mississippi Valley, Radisson found no passage to the Pacific, but instead opened the West to the pioneer fur traders who followed him.

JIM BECKWOURTH (1800–1866)
Mountain man Jim Beckwourth was a leading fur trader, Indian fighter, mail rider, mule skinner, and guide to wagon trains and cavalry. Beckwourth was the son of a white father and a mulatto mother, meaning that one of her parents was white and one was black. He was the most famous African-American frontiersmen in the West.

FRONTIER PATHFINDER
Fur trader and explorer Jedediah Smith (1799–1831) survived Indian battles, almost died of thirst during this expedition across California's Mohave Desert, and was mauled by a grizzly bear. Smith discovered important wagon routes to Oregon and California before being killed in a fight with Comanches in the Southwest.

POWDER HORNS
Hollowed-out horns that held gunpowder were tightly sealed and fitted with a strap to be slung over the mountain man's shoulder.

TRAPPER'S OTTERSKIN HAT
White trappers and frontiersmen adopted native clothing such as this ottreskin hat, worn by a mountain man.

Turkey feather

Colorful Crow-style beadwork

A RIOTOUS RENDEZVOUS
Each summer, trappers, traders, and Indians met at "rendezvous," such as this one near the Platte River. There they exchanged trade goods for fur and celebrated with horse races, gambling, feasting, and drinking; afterward, the mountain men went back to fur trapping, often broke.

THE TRAPPER'S PREY
The most important fur-bearing animal was the beaver, whose soft fur was used by the hat makers of America and Europe; from 1800 to 1850, as many as 500,000 beavers a year were killed for their pelts.

Chain attached to the spring holds down trap

Pan holds bait, and triggers steel-trap jaws

JAWS OF STEEL
When a beaver stepped into this leghold trap, the jaws sprang shut and held the animal captive until the trapper arrived to kill and skin it.

THE FOREMOST MOUNTAIN MAN
Many western explorers, writers, and military men praised Jim Bridger (1804–1881) for his achievements as a trapper, wagon-train guide, and scout; Bridger was known as the greatest mountain man of all.

PRIZED TRADE GOODS
Fur traders offered native peoples manufactured wares, such as this pre-1850 trade axe, in exchange for furs and buffalo hides. Friendship with the tribes was essential if a trader was to do business and stay alive.

HUNTER'S KNIFE
Mountain men carried large butcher knives for cleaning game and removing fur pelts.

Life on the river

BEFORE RAILROADS WERE BUILT, rivers were the most important highways to and from the distant reaches of the West. The Mississippi River's largest western tributary is the Missouri, which drains the Great Plains and the Rocky Mountains. The Snake and Columbia rivers flow through the Northwest, and the Colorado, Arkansas, and Rio Grande are key waterways in the Southwest. On these rivers early explorers journeyed in swift canoes, and later, square-prowed keelboats carried freight, furs, and trade goods. By the mid-19th century, western rivers were crowded with steam-powered paddle wheelers loaded with minerals, such as coal and iron ore, and with grain, livestock, and fruit. Handsome passenger steamboats were the royalty of river craft. They offered plush cabins and fine dining as well as gambling in well-appointed saloons. A steamboat's reputation for speed was prized, so some captains enjoyed racing other boats, even though the increased steam pressure risked boiler explosions and loss of life and vessel.

RACING FOR GLORY
"Champions of the Mississippi," a lithograph by Currier and Ives, portrays two fast steamboats racing on the Mississippi. Speed won steamboats both public praise and proud customers, but racing vessels sometimes resulted in collisions or in dangerously overheated boilers that could explode, killing passengers and crew and sinking the boats.

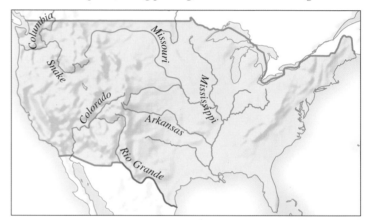

THE WEST'S GREAT RIVERS
The Mississippi and its largest tributary, the Missouri, drain much of the American West. Other major rivers include the Rio Grande and Colorado in the Southwest, and the Snake and Columbia in the Northwest.

UNDER ATTACK
Canoes, flatboats, and keelboats were common on western rivers. Flatboats, built for freight, could row into shallow waters. Keelboats had sails and moved faster, but required deeper water and could not go everywhere. Canoes were swift, but too small to carry much cargo. Indians sometimes attacked traders' flatboats, as in this incident on the Missouri.

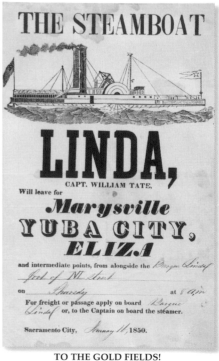

TO THE GOLD FIELDS!
In 1850, the California river steamer *Linda* advertised transportation to the gold field towns of Marysville, Yuba City, and Eliza.

FIRST-CLASS TRAVEL
A broadside advertisement from the 1870s announces service to the West by steamboat and stagecoach through northern Minnesota, Dakota, and Montana. The Northern Pacific Railroad Line carried passengers part of the way, too.

SALVAGED CHERRIES
Brandied cherries were onboard the steamboat *Bertrand*, bound from St. Louis to Montana on the Missouri River. *Bertrand* ran aground and sank in Iowa, taking the fruit with her. Years later, the cherries were salvaged and preserved as mementos of steamboat travel.

ROSEBUD
Named for the Rosebud River in Dakota Territory, this Missouri River steamboat carried soldiers and supplies during the Indian wars of the 1870s. Pictured in 1878, *Rosebud*'s usual route was between Bismarck, North Dakota, and Coalbanks, Montana, the head (or end) of navigation.

RIVERBOAT GAMBLING
Travel by riverboat became a comfortable, leisurely journey – even luxurious – and professional gamblers appeared in a boat's salon, ready to take the money of overconfident amateurs. To join in the game, players bought gambling chips worth as much as $5,000. A fortune might be won or lost on a toss of dice such as these, held by dog molds.

Smokestack

Flagstaff

Sidewheel paddle

MISSISSIPPI RIVER SIDEWHEELER
This model of the steamboat *J.M. White* shows smokestacks, passenger decks, and the side-mounted paddle wheel propulsion common to many river boats. *J.M. White*'s elegant accommodations were the finest on western waters, and she was one of the most powerful vessels of the day. She cost the enormous sum of $200,000 when built in 1878, but the rapid growth of railroads soon took away her business. *J.M. White* was destroyed by fire in 1886.

The Spanish West

SEARCHING FOR LEGENDARY CITIES OF GOLD during the 1500s, Spanish soldiers of fortune journeyed thousands of miles through the great Southwest. They returned without success to their colony of Mexico, but their explorations had opened the region to Spanish settlement. Roman Catholic priests soon established missions among the Indian tribes, who at first were oppressed by the harsh colonial government. Many priests spoke out and won the original peoples the basic right to own cattle and raise crops. Native and Spanish cultures and religions mingled to create a new people, who became independent from Spain in 1821. At this time, American settlers were establishing ranches and trading posts in the Southwest, where Santa Fe was a major commercial center. The Southwest and California were so far from governmental authority in Mexico City that they enjoyed a great deal of self-rule. Semi-independence was not enough, however, and by 1835 residents of the province of Texas were uniting to establish a new, completely independent republic.

BARTOLOME DE LAS CASAS
Sixteenth-century Dominican priest Bartolomé de Las Casas (1474–1566) worked hard to keep native peoples from being turned into slaves. Instead, slaves were brought from Africa, which Father Bartolomé regretted.

CONQUISTADOR SWORD
Until the 1700s, Spanish influence, explorations, and trade spread over a broad region that included part of the Southeast coast. This ceremonial sword, found in Georgia, is in the style of weapons carried by conquistadors, as Spanish soldiers of the time were termed.

SEARCHING FOR GOLDEN CITIES
In 1540, General Francisco de Coronado (1510–1554) headed an expedition from Mexico into the Southwest. Looking for the legendary Seven Cities of Gold, Coronado led 300 soldiers and missionaries and 800 Indians. After two years, he found no riches, but his exploration established Mexico's claim to the region.

AN EARLY MISSION
Following missionary work in the 1600s, Mission Concepción on the San Antonio River in Texas was built in the mid-1700s. The mission was built near an Indian community so the natives could be taught the Roman Catholic faith. Mission Concepción is a classical example of Spanish colonial design.

ELEGANT SHADE
Broad-brimmed Mexican felt hats are called sombreros, from the Spanish *sombra*, meaning shade. Beautifully embroidered with gold wire, this hat has a tall crown known as a sugarloaf because it looks like an old-fashioned cone of sugar.

Life in the Spanish West

The rich cultures of the New World and Old Spain mingled and thrived in the Southwest and California. Goods and handicrafts, food, clothing, tools, and agriculture – all reflected a combination of Spanish and native influences. The Roman Catholic faith also flourished and was a cornerstone of daily life. One of Spain's most outstanding contributions to the West was the introduction of the horse, which soon became prized by many Indian nations.

PRIDE OF THE HACIENDA
The Mexican love of fine horses is seen in the splendid saddle and blanket on the mount standing outside this hacienda – a country estate.

NEW MEXICAN BOX
Carved rosettes and pomegranates decorate this six-panel wooden chest made in northern New Mexico about 1800. It was used to store textiles, clothing, tools, and valuables. Spanish settlers moved into New Mexico after 1695, settling along the tributaries of the Rio Grande.

A LEATHER-JACKET SOLDIER
Mexican soldiers who wore thick leather jackets, termed *cueras*, were known as *Soldada de Cuera*, meaning "soldiers in leather jackets." These troops, who were excellent horsemen, were based at outposts throughout the Southwest and California.

La cuera

Las botas (cowhide leggings)

Patterns combine Spanish and native styles

Woolen serape, worn as a coat in Spanish America.

Wooden railings

Solid wooden wheel

STURDY OX CARTS
The dependable ox was the favored draft animal in most of the Spanish Southwest, and these wooden-wheeled carts were the most common vehicles in use. The cart required a span of two oxen; the driver walked alongside cracking a whip or switch to control the team.

Pole for team

MEXICAN FLAG
The flag of Mexico was created in 1823, after the nation won independence from Spain. The color green represents hope and fertility, white means purity, and red symbolizes the blood of patriots. Other emblems are the eagle, oak, and laurel.

MOURNING THE DEAD
The Roman Catholic faith was part of almost everyone's life – and death – in the Southwest. With the priest and altar boys in the center, a funeral procession moves slowly through the streets of San Antonio, Texas, in the early 1800s.

Struggle for the Southwest

As EARLY AS 1820, AMERICANS were settling in Texas, which belonged to Mexico, and by 1835 they numbered 25,000. The Americans and many Spanish-speaking residents of Texas wanted independence from Mexico. They united, calling themselves "Texians," and resisted Mexican rule. War broke out in 1835, and Mexico's General Santa Anna won the first battles. In 1836, his army massacred the defenders of a fortified mission at San Antonio, known as the Alamo. The dead included frontiersman Davy Crockett and Texian hero James Bowie. Santa Anna soon was defeated by Texians led by Stephen F. Austin and Sam Houston (first president of the new republic). Texas joined the United States in 1845, but Mexico objected, sparking the Mexican-American War. After a year and a half, the Americans were victorious, winning a vast territory that stretched all the way to the Pacific Ocean.

SAM HOUSTON (1793–1863)
A lawyer and former soldier, Houston was a Congressman from Tennessee before moving to Texas in the 1830s. During the rebellion against Mexico, he was commander in chief of the Texas army. In 1836, Houston was elected the first president of the Republic of Texas.

Crank for turning cylinders   *Metal grate*

COTTON GIN
The cotton gin, invented in 1793 to separate seeds from fiber, made the production of cotton extremely profitable. By the late 1820s, the East Texas plantations of American settlers used slave labor to harvest cotton, though slavery was officially banned by the Mexican government.

Wire brushes sweep cotton fibers away from saw teeth   *Circular saw disks push cotton through metal grate*

LONE STAR FLAG
This flag was adopted in 1839 by the new Republic of Texas, which was nicknamed "The Lone Star Republic."

THE BOWIE KNIFE
Invented by Texas adventurer James Bowie, this knife was meant for fighting. Its blade is 15 inches long, and its brass hand guard allows the user to parry a blow or to thrust.

The Alamo

In 1836, this mission in San Antonio was fortified to become a stronghold for rebellious "Texians." In March, a 4,000-man Mexican army attacked the Alamo and wiped out the 187 defenders. The battle cry "Remember the Alamo!" inspired Texians to win independence a year later.

DAVY CROCKETT (1786–1836)
Born in Tennessee, Crockett became a state politician, then a member of Congress. Defeated for re-election, he went to Texas, where he died at the Battle of the Alamo in 1836. Many tall tales were told about Crockett, who became a folk hero after his death.

BATTLE BEFORE WAR
General Zachary Taylor defeated Mexican forces at Palo Alto, Texas, on May 8, 1846, weeks before war was declared between the United States and Mexico. Taylor won a key victory at Buena Vista, Mexico, in February 1847.

ENTERING MEXICO CITY
Commanded by General Winfield Scott, American troops parade triumphantly in the central plaza of captured Mexico City in September 1847. This was the first time the United States raised its flag over a foreign capital. The Treaty of Guadalupe-Hidalgo in February 1848 gave the Southwest and California to the United States.

Hand guard, or "knuckle bow"

Engraved decoration

Winning California

The symbol of an independent republic, the Bear Flag was carried by American adventurers who helped United States troops capture California in 1846. The adventurers were commanded by Lieutenant John C. Frémont, the leader of surveyors mapping Oregon territory. The Americans fought not only the Mexican army, but also California volunteers who waged a brief, bitter guerrilla war against them.

The Bear Flag of the California Republic

CALIFORNIA GUERRILLAS
In June 1846, Americans living in the Mexican state of California revolted and were helped by United States soldiers. Mexican troops were defeated, but a force of hard-riding volunteer lancers courageously resisted the American invaders. The volunteers were forced to surrender in January 1847.

Scabbard

IN HONOR OF VICTORY
This sword with scabbard was presented by the people of Louisiana to General Winfield Scott for his service during the Mexican-American War. Scott commanded the American army and led the successful 1847 invasion of Mexico.

FREMONT ENTERS MONTEREY
In July 1846, explorer John Frémont led a troop of 160 Americans into Monterey, California, joining U.S. forces that had just captured the town.

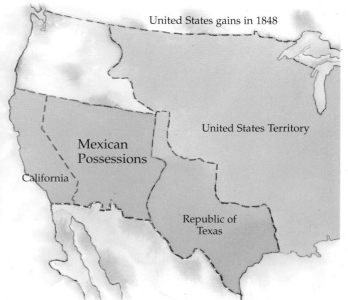

United States gains in 1848

Mexican Possessions

United States Territory

California

Republic of Texas

The miners

THE NEWS SPREAD FAST WHEN gold was discovered in 1848 at Sutter's Mill near California's Sierra Nevada mountains. Many Americans were excited by "Gold Fever," and within a year thousands of dreamers and opportunists were heading for the West Coast. Many went overland, others by ship. Known as forty-niners, the prospectors who arrived in 1849 were followed in the next ten years by 260,000 more hopefuls from many countries, including China, Peru, and Australia. Year after year, new strikes sent miners rushing around the West, from Arizona to the Dakotas, pick and shovel on their shoulders. Some found their gold in nuggets or flakes or dust, others found silver, but most gave up, defeated and broke. The lone-wolf prospector soon was replaced by hired men employed in deep, lantern-lit shafts of mines like Nevada's Comstock. Though the dream of quick wealth seldom came true, many newcomers to the West raised families and built homes that endured long after the fever had passed.

THE RUSH BEGAN HERE
In 1848, thrilling news flashed around the world that gold had been discovered at Sutter's Mill on the American River, attracting thousands of miners to California and the West.

HOW TO GET THERE
Guidebooks to the West were popular after 1850, as prospectors hungered for good advice on how to reach California.

Pan for washing gold-bearing silt

Miner's pickaxe

SLUICING THE CREEK
Forty-niners in California's Sierra Nevada mountains shovel mud from a streambed into a wooden sluice, where flowing water washes away the lighter silt, leaving gold behind.

GOLD IN THE HILLS
Veins of gold encased in solid rock were exposed by the prospector wielding pick and shovel; later, mining companies sprayed high-pressure jets of water against hillsides to reveal the gold.

Chain to suspend tray

ITS WEIGHT IN GOLD
A day's work was measured on balance scales, which were carried in a protective case; a known weight was put on one tray and gold added to the other until the two balanced, indicating the weight of the gold.

Measuring tray

Carrying case

PAYDIRT AT THEIR FEET
Men from many nations labored side by side in the gold fields. In 1852 at Auburn Ravine, California, these Americans and Chinese built their sluice on gravel banks called placers – profitable sites for finding gold dust and nuggets.

SEEING THE ELEPHANT
No one could say they had been to a circus unless they had seen the elephant. Likewise, if a forty-niner found gold in California, he could claim to have "seen the elephant," as did these prospectors pictured in an 1853 lithograph.

MINER'S LAMP
Lanterns of iron or brass lit the mine shafts that burrowed into hillsides; some lanterns burned whale oil, while others, such as this one, used candles.

DELVING FOR SILVER
Mining companies created deep-shaft works, such as this silver mine at Virginia City, Nevada, shown in cross-section; at bottom are drawings of mills where ore was refined to separate out silver.

CHILLY, WET, AND SLOW
About 1878, Dakota Territory miners slosh silt around in their shallow pans until the heavier gold dust is left. Washing gold required robust health and much patience, for the stream water was ice cold and the process tedious.

Moving West

IN THE MID-19TH CENTURY, most overland travelers moved only as fast as a team of oxen could pull a loaded wagon in a train several miles long. Much of a year was needed to reach the far West, and success required careful planning and good equipment. Many "overlanders" died along the way, and many more stopped to take up land in country that suited them well enough. The rutted trails of wagon trains were littered with cast-off possessions left behind because draft animals died or wagons broke down. In the late 1840s, the promise of religious freedom inspired thousands of Mormons to settle in Utah's isolated Salt Lake Valley. The chance for free land urged others onward through mountain passes to Oregon and across waterless deserts to California. Overlanders were not after the quick riches of gold and silver strikes. Instead, they came to work the land and build homes they would never leave again.

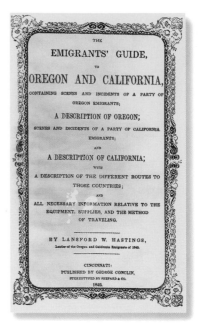

EMIGRANTS' GUIDE
Overlanders acquired instruction books with advice on crossing the country by wagon train, including what supplies and equipment were needed, and what the country was like. This 1845 book promotes Oregon and California as ideal destinations, where pioneers surely would settle happily.

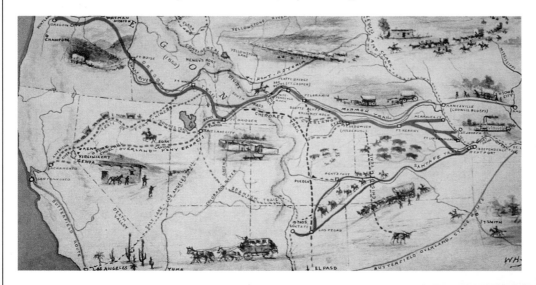

THE MANY WAYS WESTWARD
The journey across the West usually began in Missouri, and most wagon trains followed a central route, with several forks leading off from the main trail. The 2,400-mile Oregon Trail led from Independence, Missouri, to Oregon City in Oregon. Other trails turned southwest toward California or south into Utah. Routes used by stagecoaches, Pony Express, traders, and cattle drives are also indicated on this map.

CHIMNEY ROCK
Landmarks on the long trail westward told travelers where they were. One of the best known was Chimney Rock, which rises high above Nebraska's sandy Platte River country and can be seen from miles away.

A BEACON ON THE OREGON TRAIL
Thousands of emigrants on the Oregon Trail stopped at the mission of Narcissa and Dr. Marcus Whitman, near Walla Walla, Washington. Native peoples resented wagon trains and accused the Whitmans of caring about whites more than Indians. In 1847, the mission was attacked, and the Whitmans were murdered.

The Mormon Trail

The Christian denomination known as the Church of Jesus Christ of Latter-day Saints – Mormons – was one of the largest groups to migrate westward. Persecuted for their beliefs, Mormons organized traveling parties to go west. From the mid-1840s to the late 1860s, Mormon parties followed a route from Nauvoo, Illinois, along the north bank of the Platte River, and eventually to the Great Salt Lake in Utah. Some were known as "handcart companies" because they pulled handcarts instead of using horse-drawn wagons, which they could not afford. One company, with almost 3,000 persons and 655 handcarts, walked more than 1,300 miles to Utah.

Cogwheel

MEASURING MILES
Mormons invented this "roadometer" to record the miles they covered on their journey each day. Attached and geared to a cart or wagon wheel, the roadometer's toothed cogwheels measured distance as the wheel turned.

JOSEPH SMITH (1805–1844)
Vermont native Joseph Smith, founder of the Church of Jesus Christ of Latter-day Saints, inspired thousands to journey westward to practice their faith in peace. In 1844, he was murdered by an anti-Mormon mob in Illinois, and fellow Vermonter Brigham Young led the Mormons to Utah.

THE HANDCART COMPANY
In search of a homeland where they might live and worship in peace, Mormon handcart companies struggled across the West. Many believers were recently arrived from Europe, where they had been converted to the faith. The main Mormon settlements – mostly in Utah – were strengthened by the steady arrival of new handcart companies.

A WELL-DESERVED REST
While their draft animals graze, pioneers with covered wagons commonly known as Prairie Schooners pause while journeying through Utah in the 1870s. Wagon trains usually stopped at noontime, when the sun was hottest. They kept a steady pace of only ten or twelve miles a day to make sure their teams would not be worn out.

Prairie Schooner

Continued from previous page

Wagons Ho!

Setting off from Independence, Missouri, wagon trains had almost two thousand miles of grassland, dry prairie, mountain, and desert to cross before their journey would be done. The great Conestoga wagon of eastern travel was redesigned to become the "Prairie Schooner," a lighter but sturdy design adapted to the West. Weather, weariness, and hunger were the pioneer's worst adversaries, although there were clashes with Indians who stole livestock and sometimes attacked solitary wagons.

Canvas covering

THE CONESTOGA WAGON

Hoops overlaid with a canvas tarp gave the "covered wagon" its name. One of the first was the Conestoga, named for the Pennsylvania community where they were originally built. However, the huge Conestoga required a team of six horses or oxen, and carrying several thousand pounds of freight, it was far too heavy for the muddy rutted trails of the West.

Driver's box

THE PRAIRIE SCHOONER

A schooner is a small sailing ship, and the best-known overland wagon was appropriately termed the Prairie Schooner. Slowly rocking across the landscape, its canvas flapping like a sail, the light and durable wagon was generally pulled by a team of oxen. Fully loaded, Prairie Schooners weighed about 2,500 pounds. A family's survival depended on their wagon holding up in harsh weather and on stony tracks, which could shatter wheels and bend axles.

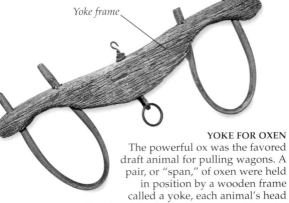

Yoke frame

YOKE FOR OXEN

The powerful ox was the favored draft animal for pulling wagons. A pair, or "span," of oxen were held in position by a wooden frame called a yoke, each animal's head passing through a hoop. Oxen were driven by someone walking alongside, touching them with a stick or cracking a whip over their heads.

A SUDDEN RAID

Attacks by Indians on wagon trains are mostly the creation of Western adventure stories and films. Yet, occasional surprise strikes by war parties did catch an isolated wagon, such as this, while its family struggled to ford a river.

PACK SADDLE

Wooden frameworks strapped to the backs of pack animals, such as horses and mules, were a secure means of transporting packages, sacks, boxes, and baskets. The horses or mules were led by hand or tethered to the back of a wagon, or behind another pack animal or a horse and rider.

Packing up

Families had to decide what to take West and what to leave. Food, tools, housewares, and a few furniture pieces filled up the wagon. Mirrors, dolls, musical instruments, or books might seem like luxuries, but often they found a place, even if family members had to walk to provide space for them.

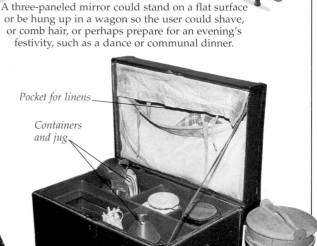

TRAVELING MIRROR
A three-paneled mirror could stand on a flat surface or be hung up in a wagon so the user could shave, or comb hair, or perhaps prepare for an evening's festivity, such as a dance or communal dinner.

ESSENTIAL CARGO
Wooden barrels were stored in wagons or hung on the outside. Barrels protected flour, bacon, salt pork, corn meal, dried beans, fruit, and hardtack (hard bread wafers) from insects, dust, and heat.

Pocket for linens

Containers and jug

BAGGED PROVISIONS
Certain foods, such as coffee, tea, sugar, rice, and salt, required the extra protection of burlap sacks, which helped keep them dry and made them easier to store.

A WELL-TRAVELED DOLL
A child's favorite doll was precious cargo, carried on even the longest journey across the West, and offering comfort when it seemed a trek would never end.

HOUSEWARES AT THE READY
Everything a cook needed to make meals was carried in a kitchen chest – everything but food. Easily lifted in and out of a wagon, the chest held cutlery, spices, jugs, and jars, even offering a pouch for tablecloths and napkins.

THE EVENING CAMPFIRE
Weathered guides and wagon drivers on the Oregon Trail settle down around a cooking fire while a fiddler strikes up a tune and late arrivals pull into camp.

Homesteading on government land

THE HOMESTEAD ACT OF 1862 offered up to 160 acres of free land to pioneers willing to live on it for at least five years. On the almost treeless plains, homesteaders used sod to build their first shelters, called "soddies." Sod bricks were about three feet long and a few inches thick. They were laid up for the walls and placed on rafter poles for the roof. The few items a family had brought out West turned a mere shelter into a home. Wooden construction would not be possible until the growth of a nearby town, where lumber and shingles would be sold. After a family had established a farm, it could afford a wood-framed home with kitchen, hearth, glazed windows, and wooden floors.

HONORING HOMESTEADERS
A 1962 stamp commemorates the national Homestead Act of 1862, which opened much of the West to settlement. The family and sod house pictured on the stamp are based on a period photograph, which was the same one used as the basis for the Norwegian emigration stamp on page 43.

PRIDE OF ACHIEVEMENT
A close look reveals how much this family has accomplished, building a home where there was only wind and prairie grass before they came. The well-made sod house can hold the weight of grazing livestock. The tall windows – or "lights" – let welcome daylight inside, but they were hard to come by on the plains. Food is on the table, a good team of working mules stands in harness, and the family shows every sign of future prosperity.

MISSOURI IS FREE!
This misleading 1870 advertisement suggests Missouri land is there for the taking. In fact, "free" likely refers to this former slave state no longer permitting slavery after the Civil War. Available land seemed endless, but was not free, costing $3-$10 an acre. In this case, land was being sold by the Hannibal and St. Joseph Railroad, which controlled it.

A KANSAS LAND OFFICE
Prospective homesteaders discuss available acreage at a land-sales office in Sedgewick County, Kansas, during the 1870s. Some study a wall map indicating the parcels of land and showing what was available and what had already been taken.

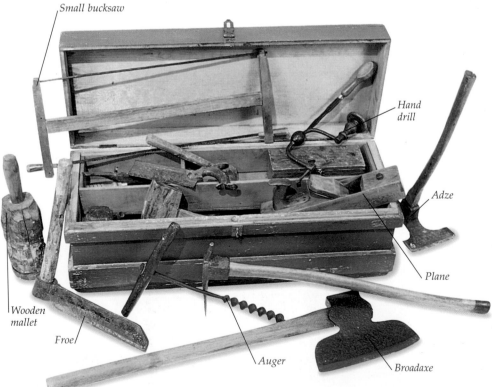

Small bucksaw

Hand drill

Adze

Plane

Wooden mallet

Froe

Auger

Broadaxe

WOODWORKING TOOLS
Carefully maintained tools were brought West in stout chests. This tool box, taken on the Oregon Trail, has a broadaxe and adze for shaping logs, augers for boring holes, and a variety of small hand tools for finishing wood and making furniture.

AT HOME BY THE STREAM
Parts of Nebraska offered settlers good homesites in groves of trees and near streams. Such sites were sought by pioneer families, who needed a ready supply of water. This Knox County family has built a log cabin beside the Niobrara River.

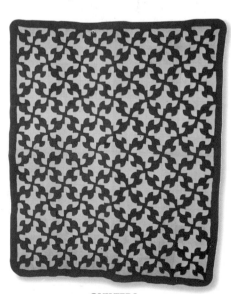

QUILTERS
Many women pioneers took special pride in skillful quilt-making. Years later, each patch could remind the maker of what was happening in her life at the time it was cut and sewn into the quilt. Made in Kentucky, this quilt was brought West by an emigrant family.

Life of a frontier family

Survival on a remote farm or ranch required hard work. Men and boys labored in the fields, pastures, and barns, while women and children prepared and preserved food, made clothes, and maintained the household. At first, store-bought goods were luxuries, so most of what was needed – from soap to butter – was produced at home. By 1870, yarn for knitting or weaving usually could be bought cheaply from the general store, yet the family spinning wheel often kept a place of honor. Once a secure home had been established, the next step was to cooperate with others in building a permanent community. Opening a school was extremely important for frontier folk, who believed education gave their children the best chance of future success.

Windmill to pump water

A VIEW OF THE PIONEER CABIN
The settler's home offered the essentials of a comfortable – if unwasteful – way of living. A shingled roof and squared logs with dried mud chinked between them meant the house was dry and tight, resistant to the harsh winters and hot summers. At first there would be just a dirt floor, but in time came a wooden floor and partition walls for small bedrooms.

COFFEE GRINDER
Most food had to be processed before it was ready to eat. For instance, grain had to be ground into flour or flakes and coffee beans had to be ground up in a mill such as this one.

OIL LAMPS
Glass-chimney lamps burned oil to light up cabins. Some lamps were of brass, others tin, and some – like this one, which once was on an elegant steamboat – were made of decorated glass.

THE HEIRLOOM SPINNING WHEEL
Store-bought thread was widely available to pioneers, but the family's spinning wheel was preserved for generations. The wheel was a cherished memento of the past. This wheel was for spinning thread out of flax.

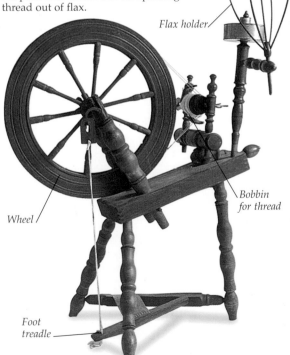
Flax holder
Bobbin for thread
Wheel
Foot treadle

KITCHEN STOVE
Though they weighed hundreds of pounds, many cast-iron stoves were hauled West. Some had to be left behind on the way, but others reached their destinations and became the centerpiece of a settler's newly built cabin.

BOXES AND SPOONS OF WOOD
This artfully fashioned woodenware set of the 1850s includes spice containers and utensils. The small boxes are labeled for the kitchen seasonings, cloves, allspice, and cinnamon, and the large box is ideal for flour.

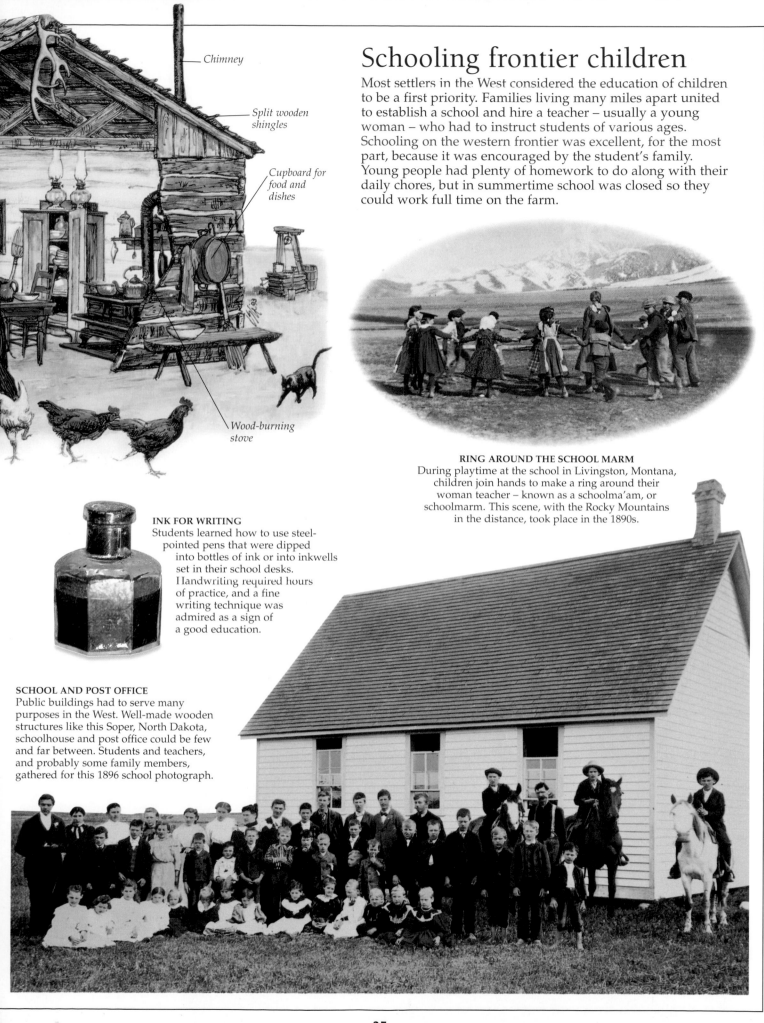

Chimney

Split wooden shingles

Cupboard for food and dishes

Wood-burning stove

Schooling frontier children

Most settlers in the West considered the education of children to be a first priority. Families living many miles apart united to establish a school and hire a teacher – usually a young woman – who had to instruct students of various ages. Schooling on the western frontier was excellent, for the most part, because it was encouraged by the student's family. Young people had plenty of homework to do along with their daily chores, but in summertime school was closed so they could work full time on the farm.

RING AROUND THE SCHOOL MARM
During playtime at the school in Livingston, Montana, children join hands to make a ring around their woman teacher – known as a schoolma'am, or schoolmarm. This scene, with the Rocky Mountains in the distance, took place in the 1890s.

INK FOR WRITING
Students learned how to use steel-pointed pens that were dipped into bottles of ink or into inkwells set in their school desks. Handwriting required hours of practice, and a fine writing technique was admired as a sign of a good education.

SCHOOL AND POST OFFICE
Public buildings had to serve many purposes in the West. Well-made wooden structures like this Soper, North Dakota, schoolhouse and post office could be few and far between. Students and teachers, and probably some family members, gathered for this 1896 school photograph.

The Pony Express

THE IMAGE OF DARING YOUNG RIDERS carrying express mail on fast ponies is one of the most enduring symbols of the West. The legendary "Pony Express" lasted only 18 months, however, ending when the transcontinental telegraph line was completed in October 1861. The firm of Russell, Majors and Waddell, which operated an overland mail and passenger service, established the Pony Express, sending its first rider from St. Joseph, Missouri, on April 3, 1860. Each horseman galloped distances of 10-15 miles between way stations, often changing horses on the run. A chain of 190 Pony Express stations provided fresh horses and riders to speed the satchel of mail on its way. Letters could be carried the 1,800 miles from Missouri to California within 10 days, half the time required by stagecoach delivery.

EXPRESS CHARGES
The Pony Express was privately run and set its own rates. A half-ounce letter cost a dollar to send from New York to San Francisco.

"THE FIRST RIDE"
Crowds gathered to watch and cheer as the first rider gallops away at the opening of Pony Express service from St. Joseph, Missouri, in 1860.

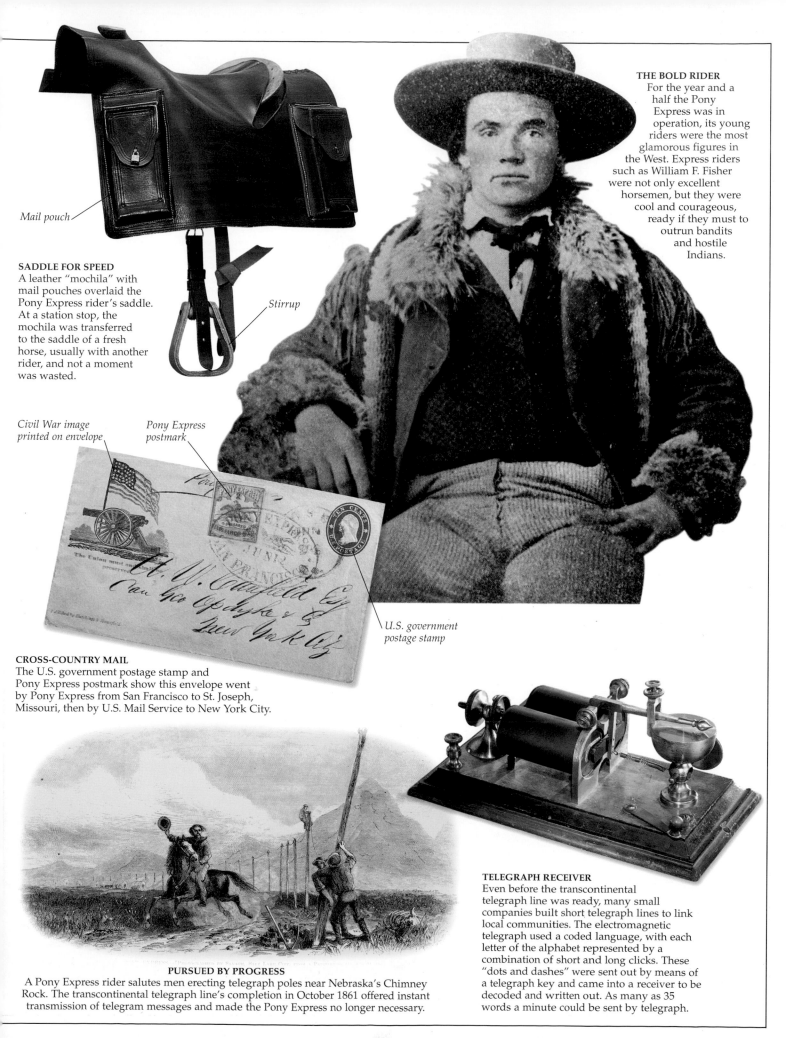

SADDLE FOR SPEED
A leather "mochila" with mail pouches overlaid the Pony Express rider's saddle. At a station stop, the mochila was transferred to the saddle of a fresh horse, usually with another rider, and not a moment was wasted.

Mail pouch

Stirrup

THE BOLD RIDER
For the year and a half the Pony Express was in operation, its young riders were the most glamorous figures in the West. Express riders such as William F. Fisher were not only excellent horsemen, but they were cool and courageous, ready if they must to outrun bandits and hostile Indians.

Civil War image printed on envelope

Pony Express postmark

U.S. government postage stamp

CROSS-COUNTRY MAIL
The U.S. government postage stamp and Pony Express postmark show this envelope went by Pony Express from San Francisco to St. Joseph, Missouri, then by U.S. Mail Service to New York City.

PURSUED BY PROGRESS
A Pony Express rider salutes men erecting telegraph poles near Nebraska's Chimney Rock. The transcontinental telegraph line's completion in October 1861 offered instant transmission of telegram messages and made the Pony Express no longer necessary.

TELEGRAPH RECEIVER
Even before the transcontinental telegraph line was ready, many small companies built short telegraph lines to link local communities. The electromagnetic telegraph used a coded language, with each letter of the alphabet represented by a combination of short and long clicks. These "dots and dashes" were sent out by means of a telegraph key and came into a receiver to be decoded and written out. As many as 35 words a minute could be sent by telegraph.

Stagecoaches

Until the coming of the railroad, stagecoaches were the fastest way to carry passengers and freight in the West. The stagecoach was built to withstand deep ruts in roads that forded streams, climbed mountains, and crossed deserts – often through rain and snow that could suddenly wipe out the track. Stagecoaches took their name from their method of traveling by short stages of ten or twenty miles between station stops. The Concord was the most popular stagecoach, a marvel of efficiency and strength. The light coach body was suspended on thick leather straps called thoroughbraces, which absorbed much of the bone-jarring shock from bad roads. The most famous stagecoach operator was Wells, Fargo & Co., known for regularly shipping valuable cargo in its strongboxes. The Post Office contracted with stagecoach companies to carry the U.S. mail. Mailbags were usually carried under the driver's seat.

FIT FOR RUGGED DUTY
The traveler's most precious possessions were tightly packed into a sturdy wooden trunk, which was cushioned inside and built to endure rough handling.

Luggage and cargo rack

Wheel spoke

Brake

WAYSIDE STATION STOP
Stagecoach lines established stations along the route, where horses were changed and passengers rested. Pulled by a fresh six-horse team, a coach draws away from the bustling Virginia Dale stage station in Colorado.

GREASE HORN
A steer horn containing grease would hang between the wheels of the stagecoach. The grease was used to lubricate the axles.

MILITARY ESCORT
This Concord Coach, pictured around 1869, has a military escort. Soldiers often guarded express company stagecoaches carrying valuable freight or mail.

BLACK BART
Between 1875 and 1883, a robber nicknamed "Black Bart" held up 28 California stagecoaches. Charles E. Boles (1830–1917?) was captured after accidentally dropping a handkerchief with laundry markings that identified him as Black Bart.

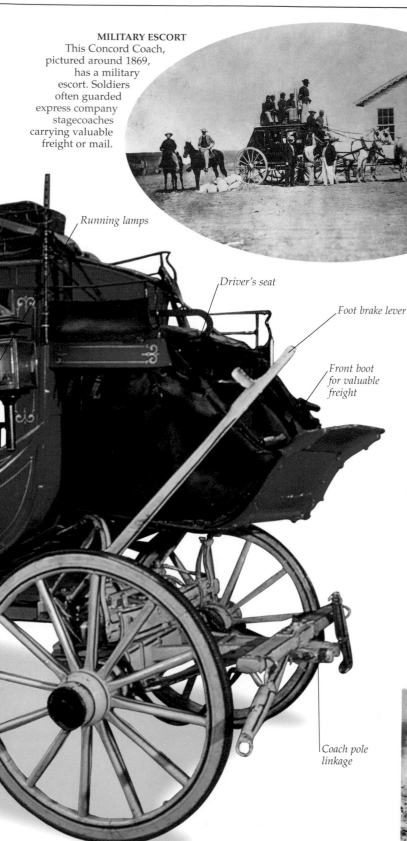

Running lamps

Driver's seat

Foot brake lever

Front boot for valuable freight

Coach pole linkage

DOWNING THE LEADER
Contemporary artist Frederic Remington (1861–1909) pictured how an Indian attack on a racing stagecoach might succeed – by killing one of the team. There were few such attacks on stagecoaches, which took routes that steered clear of hostile territory.

THE OVERLAND STAGE
Named after the town in New Hampshire where it was built, this Concord stagecoach owned by Wells, Fargo is light but durable. Its large wheels kept the coach out of the mud and above deep ruts. Wells, Fargo's stagecoaches, which were extremely well-maintained, weighed 2,500 pounds, and seated nine passengers.

THE LONELY TRAIL
The stagecoach driver, sometimes called a reinsman, has to be on the alert for washed-out roads as his team picks its way down a narrow mountain pass.

Railroads span the continent

THE FIRST TRANSCONTINENTAL RAILROAD, a slender thread of steel joining the western coast to the cities of the Midwest, was completed in 1869. Within ten years, railroads were booming, and no other single factor would do so much, so fast, to develop and change the West. While bringing rapid settlement and progress to farming, cattle, and mining regions, the railroad also doomed the way of life of the native peoples. The buffalo that the nations depended upon were driven toward extinction, as professional hide-hunters operating from railroad depots destroyed the beasts by the millions. Nor could the Indian warrior on horseback match the swift movement of soldiers on the "Iron Horse," as they named the locomotive. Also conquered by the railroad were the great distances and difficult terrain of the West. By 1890, even the most demanding traveler was crossing the continent in speed, style, and comfort.

STRAIGHT TO THE HORIZON
With visitors looking on, a Chinese work gang for the Central Pacific Railway lays track across the desert in the mid-1860s. The earth for the roadbed was shaped, then wooden cross-ties laid, and iron rails were placed on top. Spikes were hammered into the wood to clamp the rails in place.

PROUD JUPITER
Jupiter was one of the locomotives in the 1869 ceremony at Promontory, Utah. Powered by steam, she used wood for fuel, which was carried in the tender behind the engine. Central Pacific enginemen took great pride in Jupiter, polishing her brass and keeping her paint fresh. The "cowcatcher" framework in front is designed to push debris – even cows – out of the way of the moving train.

Smokestack

Coal-oil burning headlamp

Whistle

Tender for wood or coal

Pilot, or "Cowcatcher"

TRAVELING BAG
Buffalo-hide bags were popular with doctors, salesmen, and travelers in the 19th century. The top-break style made these bags easy to open and close. The wide use of buffalo hide for bags and blankets – and especially for leather conveyor belts in factories – led to slaughter of the herds.

FIRST-CLASS LUXURY
In the mid-1860s, Chicago industrialist George Pullman developed a railroad car with seats that converted into beds. The Chicago and Alton Rail Road's advertising promised that the Pullman sleeping car was the most comfortable way to travel overland.

PROMONTORY, UTAH
Some Chinese immigrants, many of whom came to the United States for the California gold rush, found work on the railroads. This Chinese tracklaying crew was photographed at Promontory, Utah, in 1869. Because of prejudice and pressure from white labor unions, this stream of cheap labor was cut off in 1882 when Congress banned virtually all immigration from China.

ONE–DOLLAR WATCH
This inexpensively made silver-plated railroad pocket watch with a picture of a train on the cover was known as a "one-dollar watch."

SPANNING THE CONTINENT
The Union Pacific railroad, coming from the East, and the Central Pacific, from the West, laid track until they met at Promontory, near Ogden, Utah. A ceremony was held May 10, 1869, as the last section of rail was laid. Brought nose to nose – cowcatcher to cowcatcher – the UP locomotive is on the right, the CP locomotive on the left.

Postage stamp to commemorate the transcontinental railroad

DESTINATION SAN FRANCISCO
In 1869, the Union Pacific railroad company promoted travel by train to California. This announcement reads, "Omaha…Through to San Francisco in less than Four Days, avoiding the Dangers of the Sea!"

SYMBOL OF SUCCESS
A golden spike was made to celebrate the completion of the transcontinental railroad track. While photographers took pictures, officials pretended to hammer the spike into the last cross-tie. The golden spike was later replaced with one made of ordinary iron.

Frontier melting pot

ONE-THIRD OF THOSE WHO CAME TO THE WEST between 1846 and 1880 were foreign-born. Most wanted only to farm good land and to raise families. Others, such as the German-Russian Mennonites, were seeking religious freedom. St. Louis had a large German population, Minnesota and Wisconsin had many Scandinavians, and California had dynamic Chinese and Japanese communities. In 1870, the Irish-born accounted for one in four of California's population, and Italians and Portuguese also were numerous on the West Coast. Native peoples remained an important part of western culture, just as Mexican-Americans were the majority in the Southwest and southern California. After the Civil War, thousands of black families journeyed westward, determined to make the most of their recent liberty.

PEOPLES OF THE WORLD
A railroad platform on the Union Pacific line in 1869 teems with travelers, rich and poor, from many lands and cultures. The station is mobbed with Europeans, African-Americans, Chinese, Native Americans, and assorted prospectors, speculators, investors, game hunters, and soldiers.

The Chinese

With the discovery of California gold in 1848, Chinese adventurers began to come by the thousands to the land they called "Gold Mountain." Many found work in gold mines and in railroad construction, while others started businesses. At first, there was much prejudice against them because their language and culture was not understood. In time, the Chinese made their own place in the American West, paving the way for other Asians to come to the United States.

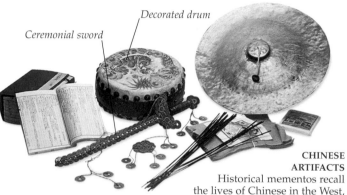

Ceremonial sword   *Decorated drum*

CHINESE ARTIFACTS
Historical mementos recall the lives of Chinese in the West, including drums, incense, temple hangings, books, and fireworks. Such items helped Chinese maintain a sense of community and continuing culture.

CHAMPION FIREMEN
Nothing was more thrilling to westerners than competitions matching fire departments and hose teams against one another. This immaculately uniformed group of young Chinese-American firemen won the hose team race held at Deadwood, Dakota, on July 4, 1888.

African-Americans

Several African-Americans were among the first mountain men and pioneers in the West. After the Civil War, young black men served in the cavalry and infantry during the Indian wars, while others became expert cowboys. Thousands of former slaves emigrated westward from the plantations in the South into the new lands to take up farms in Kansas, Nebraska, and Oklahoma, where blacks would found their own university. Others journeyed farther west to the mountain states and the West Coast, establishing homes and businesses in cities such as Denver and San Francisco.

Ho for Kansas!

Brethren, Friends, & Fellow Citizens:
I feel thankful to inform you that the

REAL ESTATE
AND
Homestead Association,
Will Leave Here the

15th of April, 1878,

In pursuit of Homes in the Southwestern Lands of America, at Transportation Rates, cheaper than ever was known before.

For full information inquire of Benj. Singleton, better known as old Pap, NO. 5 NORTH FRONT STREET.

Beware of Speculators and Adventurers, as it is a dangerous thing to fall in their hands.

Nashville, Tenn., March 18, 1878.

HO FOR KANSAS!
This 1878 poster, bearing the name of former slave Benjamin "Pap" Singleton as the promoter, invites blacks from Tennessee to come to Kansas and homestead.

A HOME ON FREE SOIL
Moses Speese and family sit for a photographer in Custer County, Nebraska, in 1888. By the end of the century, black farmers were working more than 50,000 acres in Nebraska.

Russians, Scandinavians, and Germans

German-Russian Mennonites, seeking religious freedom, brought their centuries-long tradition of wheat farming to Kansas. Wheat from their homeland thrived in the West and became a profitable crop. Scandinavians and Germans also were important settlers, many owning farms or working in the lumber trade. One emigrant office in Scandinavia sent 10,000 folk from Denmark, Sweden, and Norway to Nebraska. An agent claimed to have brought 60,000 Germans to Kansas alone.

QUILTING AND SONG
In the 1890s, North Dakotans of Norwegian descent pose for a photograph that shows their favorite pastimes: the women are making quilts or patchwork, a foot-treadled sewing machine between them, while the man entertains them with his guitar.

RUSSIAN MENNONITE BARRACKS
Central Kansas had colonies of German-Russians who practiced the Mennonite faith, for which they had been persecuted in their native Russia. At first, they raised large barracks and lived communally, but in time each family built its own home: first dugouts with sod walls and roofs, later log cabins, and eventually fine houses on sprawling, prosperous farms.

UTVANDRINGEN TIL AMERIKA
"Emigration to America," reads this 1975 Norwegian stamp honoring the Norwegians who came to the New World. Many made their first homes in dugout soddies on the Great Plains.

NORGE — UTVANDRINGEN TIL AMERIKA — 125

The cavalrymen

SINCE WELL BEFORE THE MEXICAN WAR of 1846–1848, hard-riding mounted infantry, called dragoons, were stationed in the American West. At first they protected wagon trains crossing to California and Oregon or they garrisoned remote outposts to keep watch on Indian country. After the Civil War, dragoons were replaced by cavalrymen who seemed born to the saddle, riding out on long-range patrols or suddenly striking in force. The lean, tough cavalryman often was the only peacekeeper for hundreds of miles around his fort. Now he was guarding the construction of new railroads and telegraph lines as well as protecting gold miners in Montana and Nevada and survey parties taking measurements in every region of the West. Indian-fighting was the troopers' most difficult duty, but boredom in isolated forts was especially hard on these men, soldiers in a wild and lonely land.

A TOKEN OF SERVICE
The army awarded cavalrymen a medal to commemorate their years of campaigning during the Indian Wars from 1870 to 1890.

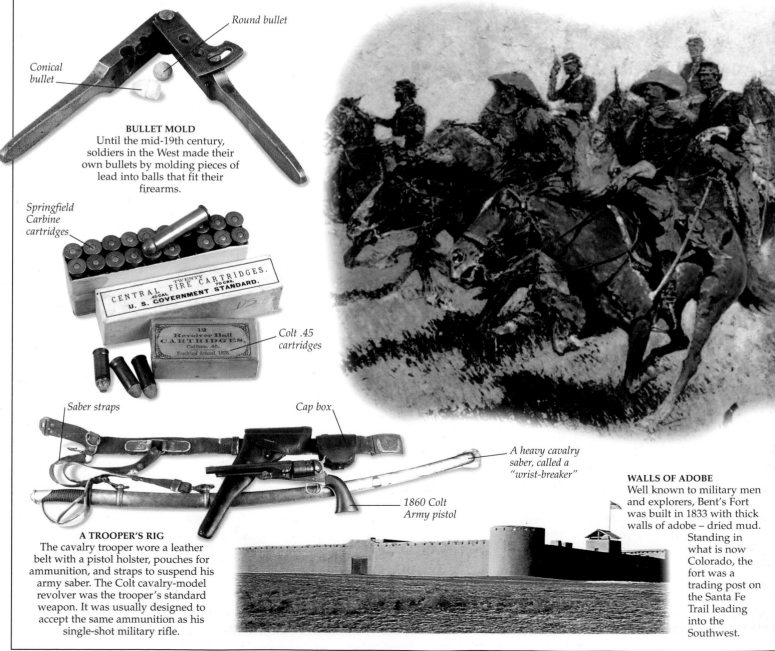

Round bullet

Conical bullet

BULLET MOLD
Until the mid-19th century, soldiers in the West made their own bullets by molding pieces of lead into balls that fit their firearms.

Springfield Carbine cartridges

TWENTY
CENTRAL FIRE CARTRIDGES.
.45 CAL. 70 GRS.
U. S. GOVERNMENT STANDARD.

12
Revolver Ball
CARTRIDGES,
Calibre .45.
Frankford Arsenal, 1878.

Colt .45 cartridges

Saber straps

Cap box

A heavy cavalry saber, called a "wrist-breaker"

1860 Colt Army pistol

A TROOPER'S RIG
The cavalry trooper wore a leather belt with a pistol holster, pouches for ammunition, and straps to suspend his army saber. The Colt cavalry-model revolver was the trooper's standard weapon. It was usually designed to accept the same ammunition as his single-shot military rifle.

WALLS OF ADOBE
Well known to military men and explorers, Bent's Fort was built in 1833 with thick walls of adobe – dried mud. Standing in what is now Colorado, the fort was a trading post on the Santa Fe Trail leading into the Southwest.

A SAFE HAVEN
Set on the northern plains, Fort Laramie protected wagon trains traveling along the Oregon Trail, as seen in this 1860 painting. The fort was built by fur traders in 1834 and sold to the U.S. government for a military post in 1849; it remained in use until 1890.

CAVALRY PENNANT
Cavalry regiments had 12 companies, each with a pennant – or "guidon" – of stars and stripes to indicate the company's position on the battlefield.

SWIFT, BOLD, AND DEADLY
Blue-coated troopers thunder across the southern plains in "The Cavalry Charge," an 1890s painting by period artist Frederic Remington. These horse-soldiers were a match for any opponent in the West, maintaining law and order in a dangerous and lawless land.

1881 Helmet

1872 Full-dress sergeant's uniform

Buffalo soldiers

After the Civil War, two regiments of black troopers (the 9th and 10th U.S. Cavalry) served in the West, fighting hostile warriors, outlaws, and border desperadoes. Indians termed them "buffalo soldiers" because of their tightly curled hair, and their toughness.

Cavalry Gauntlets

Indian wars – a century of struggle

WHITES MIGRATING WESTWARD REGULARLY CLASHED with Native Americans, who were forced to move farther and farther west. Then a Sioux uprising in 1862 drove thousands of settlers out of Minnesota, warning of even worse fighting to come. The many white-Indian conflicts during the 1880s involved almost every nation, from the Southwest Apache to the Yakima of Oregon. In 1876, warriors and soldiers fought to a draw at Rosebud Creek, Montana, and soon afterward, several nations allied to wipe out a cavalry force at the Little Big Horn River, also in Montana. This was the greatest Indian victory, but thousands more soldiers were sent against them, and most tribes had no choice but to surrender. In 1890, soldiers surrounded a group of armed Sioux at Wounded Knee Creek in South Dakota, and firing began. Almost 200 Sioux men, women, and children were killed or injured at Wounded Knee, the last battle of the Indian wars.

DRIVEN OUT
White settlers in southern Minnesota fled their homes after fierce attacks by the Santee Sioux in 1862. Before the uprising was defeated by a powerful military force, as many as 800 civilians and soldiers had been killed.

SIOUX WAR CLUB
Fashioned of elk horn, this war club resembles a water bird, with two copper disks for eyes. Artist George Catlin collected the club on an 1830s trip across the Great Plains.

PROLOGUE TO CUSTER
More than 1,200 U.S. infantry and cavalry barely avoided defeat by an equal force of Cheyenne and Sioux at the Rosebud River, Montana, in mid-June 1876. A few days later, these warriors were at the Little Big Horn and helped wipe out Custer's command.

MAKING A STAND
Surrounded by 600 Sioux and Cheyenne, 50 frontiersmen forted up on Beecher's Island, Colorado, in 1868. The defenders fought off three massed charges, killing Cheyenne war chief, Roman Nose. The frontiersmen seemed doomed until black troopers of the 10th Cavalry rode in to the rescue.

THE VICTOR'S POINT OF VIEW
In this pictograph, Sioux chief Red Horse illustrated the 1876 destruction of Lieutenant Colonel George A. Custer's 264-man 7th Cavalry detachment. Red Horse commanded warriors at this most famous battle of the Indian wars, fought near the Little Big Horn in Montana.

Lever to load bullets into firing chamber — *Hammer* — *Wooden stock*

Winchester carbine carried by a native warrior at Little Big Horn

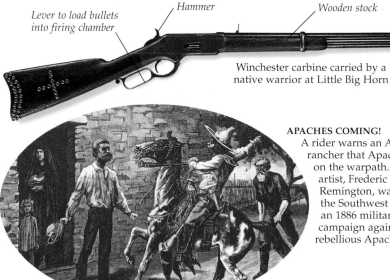

APACHES COMING!
A rider warns an Arizona rancher that Apaches are on the warpath. The artist, Frederic Remington, was in the Southwest during an 1886 military campaign against the rebellious Apache.

Moon symbol — *Fringes*

White muslin cloth

GHOST DANCE SHIRT
In 1890, many Indians were inspired by the Ghost Dance movement, which promised the triumph of native culture. Followers carried symbols of suns, moons, and stars, believed to offer protection, and wore white "Ghost Shirts" painted with these symbols.

Wounded Knee

The last "battle" of the Indian wars was the 1890 massacre of Sioux men, women, and children at Wounded Knee Creek, South Dakota. American soldiers were attempting to disarm the Sioux when firing broke out, causing almost 200 Indian and 64 soldier casualties. Yearly events at the site commemorate Wounded Knee.

MASS GRAVE
Soldiers look on as civilian grave diggers place the bodies of dead Sioux in a burial pit after the Wounded Knee Massacre.

The 1994 reenactment of Wounded Knee

Leaders of the Indian wars

THE GOVERNMENT SENT ITS BEST officers against the Indian nations, including Lieutenant Colonel George A. Custer and General George Crook. Both had commanded Union troops during the Civil War, as had frontiersman Kit Carson, leader of Union forces in the Southwest. Native chiefs had no such military experience, yet many proved to be great war leaders. Sitting Bull had been a war chief in his youth, but he later became a holy man who inspired the Sioux to defend themselves. Chief Joseph of the Nez Perces opposed war until his people were so oppressed by the government that they rebelled. Quanah Parker was a fine Comanche war chief but, like the other tribal leaders, he could not defeat the better-equipped soldiers. In 1886, General Crook hunted down the Apache medicine man, Geronimo, the last Indian to surrender to the government. Geronimo demanded to be considered not a renegade – a rebel who rejects his own people – but a prisoner of war.

GALLANT, BUT RECKLESS
This portrait of George A. Custer was painted by Alexander Lawrie c. 1876.

George A. Custer

Cavalry leader George Armstrong Custer (1839–1876) disobeyed orders in 1876 and recklessly attacked a huge Indian village near the Little Big Horn River. Custer's command was destroyed to the last man, shocking the nation, which considered him a fallen hero. Custer received many tributes, such as "Requiem to the Memory of Gen. Geo. A. Custer," music composed in his honor – and which used his Civil War rank.

Custer songsheet

Custer's buckskin campaign coat

Military buttons

Decorative fringe

CUSTER'S OFFICERS
Thirty-eight members of Lieutenant Colonel George A. Custer's officer and scientific corps pose for a group portrait at camp on Box Elder Creek, Dakota Territory, in 1874. Two years later, half of these men would die at the Little Big Horn.

Decorative knife handle

Sitting Bull's knife

Sitting Bull

A Lakota Sioux war leader in his youth, Tatanka Iyotake – Sitting Bull (c.1831–1890) – later became a head chief and holy man. After his people helped defeat Custer in 1876, Sitting Bull became famous. In 1885, he joined Buffalo Bill's Wild West Show. He was killed in 1890 during a scuffle with Indian reservation police. After his death, Sitting Bull's personal possessions were treasured as artifacts of a bygone age.

Sitting Bull's moccasins

KIT CARSON (1809–1868)
A mountain man, rancher, and soldier, Kit Carson led campaigns that subdued the Southwest's Navaho, Mescalero Apache, and Kiowa. As the Indian agent representing the government to the tribes of northern New Mexico, Carson won their trust and respect.

CHIEF JOSEPH (1840–1904)
"Thunder Rolling from the Mountains" was the native name of this pacifist Nez Perces chief who refused to be forced onto a smaller reservation. In 1877, Joseph led 350 of his people in a flight of 1,200 miles before being captured by the army.

QUANAH PARKER (c.1845–1911)
Son of a white captive and a Comanche, Quanah Parker was a war chief who, in 1875, led his Comanche band onto the Oklahoma reservation. When these Indian lands were opened to settlement in 1889, Quanah Parker bargained hard to get his people the best terms possible.

THE BEST GENERAL
Aware that "Indian troubles" were the result of broken government promises, General George Crook (1828–1890) tried diplomacy first, warfare second. A champion of native rights, Crook pacified the Northwest and the Southwest. He was considered the army's finest commander in the Indian wars.

Elusive Apache fighters

Chiricahua Apache leader Geronimo stands with some of his 50-member band of fighters near the U.S.-Mexico border in 1886. Thousands of soldiers tried to capture Geronimo, but it was the army's Apache scouts who finally tracked him down. Also helping the military were Indian police, who were sworn in as deputy sheriffs and maintained law and order on the reservations.

Apache police badge

Ammunition belt

Repeating rifle

Apache head band

Geronimo

49

Outlaws and lawmen

UNTIL THE EARLY 1890s, criminal gangs ranged throughout the West, rustling cattle, robbing small-town banks, and holding up stagecoaches and trains. Taking on outlaws required fearless gunmen like Wild Bill Hickok, the most famous lawman of the time. Some appointed peacekeepers lived, themselves, on the edge of the law. In the rough cattle town of Dodge City, the "peace commissioners" included notorious gamblers and gunfighters Luke Short and the Earp brothers. "Judge" Roy Bean, a Texas saloonkeeper and self-appointed justice of the peace, promoted illegal boxing matches and was known to interrupt his court cases to sell liquor. In spite of the romantic legends, even the best-known outlaws usually ended up in prison. Many, like young New Mexican gunslinger Billy the Kid, suffered an early and violent death. The last famous gang was Wyoming Territory's "Wild Bunch," specialists in train robbery until they were hunted down by another kind of specialist — Allan Pinkerton's detective agency.

GUIDE, GUNMAN, AND FRONTIER MARSHALL
James Butler "Wild Bill" Hickok (1837–1876) was a hunting expedition guide, a brilliant pistol shot, and a lawman in rough cattle towns. Sporting long, curly hair, Hickok acted in a Wild West show and on stage – playing himself. He was shot in the back in the mining town of Deadwood, Dakota Territory.

BADGE OF AUTHORITY
The sheriff was the elected peacekeeper in most western communities. The badge he wore was a symbol of authority and of his community's respect for him.

Sheriff's jailhouse keys

Early nickel Hiatt handcuffs

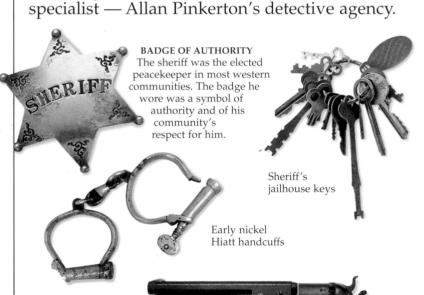

Luke Short
Wyatt Earp
Bat Masterson

THE PEACE COMMISSIONERS
To maintain law and order, frontier towns hired two-fisted gunfighters who were as tough and hot-tempered as most troublemakers. These 1870s Dodge City, Kansas, "peace commissioners" were led by gunmen Wyatt Earp, Luke Short, and Bat Masterson.

TOOLS OF THE TRADE
The Colt .36-caliber Navy Model six-shooter used a percussion cap – a small charge of gunpowder that exploded when the trigger was pulled and ignited the cartridge with the bullet. The Navy Model was replaced by the 1873 Single Action Army, which fired a metallic cartridge that did not need a percussion cap.

Gunpowder flask

Percussion caps

Tin of percussion caps

LAW WEST OF THE PECOS
In the 1880s, "Judge" Roy Bean (1825–1903) opened a saloon in West Texas on the Pecos River and declared himself justice of the peace. Pictured here trying a horse thief, Bean was respected for his common-sense handling of cases – although some decisions favored his friends.

BILLY THE KID
Legendary gunman William H. Bonney (1859–1881), nicknamed Billy the Kid, was only 17 when he killed his first man. The Kid took part in bloody feuds and crime sprees in the Southwest and was shot down by a sheriff who once had been a friend.

RAILROAD ROBBERY
Trains chugging through desolate country were targets for outlaws who blocked the track, robbed passengers, and raided the mail coach. In this 1887 hold-up of a Union Pacific train, thieves break open strongboxes for the valuables stored inside.

UNDER LOCK AND KEY
Thick-walled steel railroad safes held cash, jewelry, and gold dust which attracted bandits, who often blasted open safe doors with a charge of dynamite.

Detectives and offices　　*Symbol of alert investigators*　　*Agency slogan*

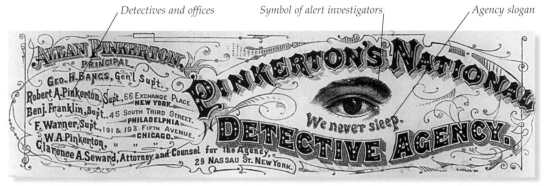

ALLAN PINKERTON, PRINCIPAL.
GEO. H. BANGS, Gen'l Supt.
Robert A. Pinkerton, Supt. 66 EXCHANGE PLACE, NEW YORK.
Benj. Franklin, Supt. 45 SOUTH THIRD STREET, PHILADELPHIA.
F. Warner, Supt. 191 & 193 FIFTH AVENUE.
W. A. Pinkerton, " CHICAGO.
Clarence A. Seward, Attorney and Counsel for the Agency, 29 NASSAU ST. NEW YORK.

PINKERTON'S NATIONAL DETECTIVE AGENCY.
We never sleep.

WE NEVER SLEEP
This advertisement bears the famous logo of the Pinkerton Detective Agency, established by Scottish immigrant Alan Pinkerton in the 1850s. As well known as any outlaw gang, Pinkerton's agency had offices in several western cities. Its detectives were admired by law-abiding folk and dreaded by criminals.

.41 caliber rimfire short cartridge

Colt "Thuer" 3rd model single-shot deringer

Harry Longbaugh "The Sundance Kid"

The Wild Bunch outlaw gang

Will Carver

Ben Kilpatrick "The Tall Texan"

Harvey Logan "Kid Curry"

Robert L. Parker "Butch Cassidy"

ENJOYING THEIR LOOT
Notorious for robbing trains and banks from Wyoming to New Mexico, the gang known as the "Wild Bunch" poses in Fort Worth, Texas, in 1901. Leaders Robert L. Parker (alias Butch Cassidy) and Harry Longbaugh (alias Sundance Kid) fled from railroad detectives and went to South America to continue their criminal careers.

Boom towns

Sᴇᴛᴛʟᴇᴍᴇɴᴛs ᴛʜᴀᴛ ᴀᴘᴘᴇᴀʀᴇᴅ sᴜᴅᴅᴇɴʟʏ and grew phenomenally fast were known as "boom towns." Many went from boom to bust in just a matter of months. Some served gold or silver mines, others were railroad terminals where cattle were shipped to market, and still others supplied lumberjacks and milled timber into lumber. When precious metals petered out, or a better railhead opened, or if the trees had been cut, the people moved on. After a few years, all that remained was a ghost town, with a lonely cemetery. Once-thriving mining settlements such as Virginia City, Montana, and Bodie, California, became ghost towns. Kansas cattle towns, Dodge City and Abilene, managed to survive, and San Francisco and Denver grew from boom towns into great metropolises.

THE RAILHEAD
A new railroad depot would turn a once-sleepy frontier settlement into a boom town, where Longhorns were herded into cattle cars for shipment to market.

SADDLE-MAKER'S TOOLS
These leather-working tools were used to make, repair, and decorate saddles. When a trail herd arrived in a cattle town, the cowboys were always in need of a saddle-maker's services to restore worn gear or to make a new saddle.

The Wild West saloon

Saloons were great attractions to the trail-weary cowboys or newly wealthy miners who came to town for a rowdy time. Patrons gambled at the card games of faro, poker, and blackjack. Liquor was sold from bottles kept on the wall behind the bar, and the air was always thick with tobacco smoke.

Back-bar bottles

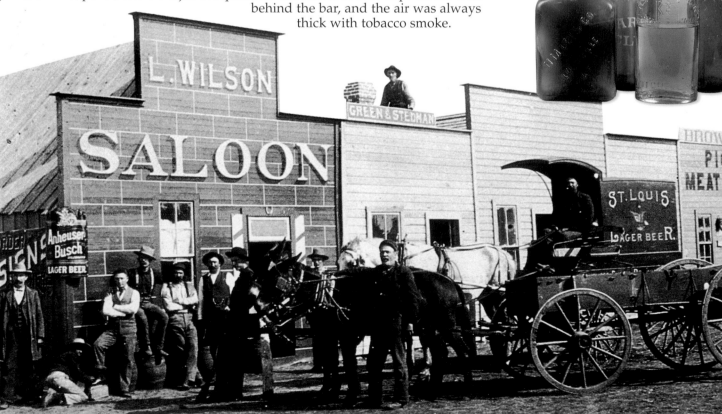

BODIE'S BOOM TO BUST
In four short years late in the 1870s, Bodie, California, went from a thriving silver-mining town to a virtual ghost town when the miners moved on to better diggings. At its peak, Bodie had 10,000 inhabitants, 2,000 buildings, and 65 saloons. Mills Street, pictured here, was a busy place. Surrounded by desert, Bodie had little to offer when the silver lode ran out.

BLAKE STREET, DENVER
Prosperity abounds on this main thoroughfare in Denver, Colorado, around the time of the Civil War. Denver had rebounded from major floods and fires that destroyed most of its original buildings. Even such calamities did not discourage the adventurers, merchants, and gold miners who swarmed to Denver, which became the largest city between St. Louis and California.

AN ABANDONED SCHOOLHOUSE
Hopes were high for a lasting community when the settlers of Calico, California, built this schoolhouse for their children. The people all departed, however, leaving the settlement a ghost town, its schoolhouse empty.

DODGE CITY IN 1878
Perhaps the most famous boom town of the West, Dodge City prospered as a Kansas cattle town after the Civil War. Dodge was known for its tough gunfighter-law officers, such as Wyatt Earp, Bat Masterson, and Bill Tilghman. Their fearsome reputations often were enough to keep the peace in saloons and on the streets with no need for gunplay.

Good doctors and snake oil salesmen

MANY WESTERN DOCTORS HAD NO FORMAL training, so they learned from experience and from books with do-it-yourself medical advice. It was the same in most of the United States, which had very few medical schools. Trained or not, good doctors were conscientious and hard-working, riding long distances from home to home to tend the sick. Often, they were paid by barter, earning chickens or fruit or firewood from their cash-poor patients. Usually, doctors were called in only for serious injuries or for illnesses that were not curable by home remedies such as a spoonful of sulphur and molasses or a dose of birch sap. Many folk favored "patent medicines," as commercially made elixirs, drops, salves, compounds, balms, liniments, and other mixtures were termed. Some so-called doctors traveled around the country selling patent medicine from wagons and advertising their wares as old Indian cures.

THE COUNTRY DOCTOR
His horse saddled and ready to continue his visits, a country doctor consults with a concerned woman, perhaps prescribing medicine for a sick family member.

Mortar

Pestle

GRINDING AND MIXING
Mortars and pestles were used to grind everything from grain to herbs to prepare a doctor's remedy for patients. Drugs, minerals, plant extracts, herbs, and dried barks were ground to a fine powder then mixed according to the doctor's prescription.

Pouch

DR. WHITMAN'S SADDLEBAGS
Dr. Marcus Whitman (1802–1847) of Oregon country was the ideal example of the tireless western doctor. Whitman rode hundreds of miles on horseback for weeks at a time visiting folk of every race. His saddlebags held medical instruments and medicines, carried through all kinds of weather, from Indian villages to white settlements and to passing wagon trains.

A physician's spectacles and case

A DOCTOR'S REMEDIES
Basic remedies prescribed by the frontier doctor included calomel, a strong laxative to cleanse the bowels, and ipecac, used to bring on vomiting. Also commonly found on physicians' shelves were morphine to numb pain, quinine for malaria, and camphor to be used as a stimulant or liniment.

THE DENTIST'S OFFICE
Dr. Greene Vardiman Black, whose bust stands in this replica of his 1885 office, is known as "The Father of Modern Dentistry." Black was a researcher and professor of dentistry in Illinois and Missouri colleges. He wrote many important papers on dentistry, and developed improved methods of cavity preparation and filling.

Snake oil salesmen

After a "medicine wagon" performance, bottles of so-called elixir were sold to audience members who had been convinced. There were medicines of all kinds, including "blood purifiers," said to cure everything from coughs and gland swellings to epilepsy and even cancer. Recipes were secret, but some contained alcohol, and many were useless. Those who doubted these medicines referred to them as "snake oil."

PLUMP AND HEALTHY
A spoon of Grove's Tasteless Chill Tonic, taken regularly, was supposed to fatten up both adults and children – making them as robust "as pigs." Chubbiness was considered a sign of good health, and the manufacturer claimed more than 20 years of success.

FOR THE LIVER
Internal disorders often were traced, rightly or wrongly, to the liver, and bottled liver cures were considered important medicine to keep on hand.

INDIAN REMEDIES
Traditional remedies used by native peoples won a reputation for being able to cure almost any illness. This 1890 "Kickapoo Indian" traveling medicine show provided lively, entertaining speeches testifying to the powers of so-called Kickapoo medicine.

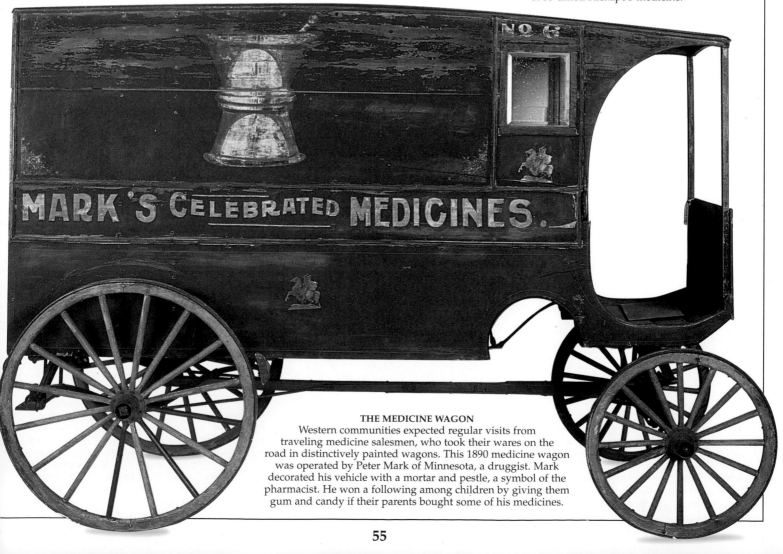

THE MEDICINE WAGON
Western communities expected regular visits from traveling medicine salesmen, who took their wares on the road in distinctively painted wagons. This 1890 medicine wagon was operated by Peter Mark of Minnesota, a druggist. Mark decorated his vehicle with a mortar and pestle, a symbol of the pharmacist. He won a following among children by giving them gum and candy if their parents bought some of his medicines.

A cowboy's life

California-style saddle

Collarless shirt

THE MOST ROMANTIC FIGURE of the Old West was the cowboy, yet his daily life was anything but romantic. It was hard, dirty, and dangerous. He worked for low pay and spent long, lonely hours in the saddle. Cowboys had to be brilliant riders, skilled with the lariat, and able to flip a steer onto its side to apply the hot branding iron. There were deadly moments, too, such as when hundreds of longhorn steers, spooked by lightning, stampeded blindly. The cowboy's only real rest was in those few off-duty hours after a spare but welcome meal at the chuck wagon. Then, men sat around the fire or in the bunkhouse, exchanging stories and singing songs, enjoying the companionship of others who, each day, shared the same hardships and dangers.

THE COWBOY'S TALE
With his 1885 book, *A Texas Cowboy*, Charles Siringo was one of the first to write about life as a cowboy. He was also a detective and a participant in range wars between sheepmen and cattlemen.

Leather waistcoat

Dressed for work

This cowboy wears showy gear, more like a rodeo performer than a working cowpuncher. Yet, each piece of clothing has a practical purpose and was essential to the Old West's cowboys. Chaps protect legs from sharp branches and cactus needles, and the broad-brimmed hat is needed against the sun and rain.

Batwing chaps

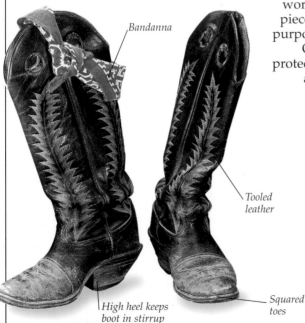

Bandanna

Tooled leather

High heel keeps boot in stirrup

Squared toes

RIDING BOOTS
Dress riding boots were often beautifully decorated and of top-grade leather. Working cowboys favored plain boots with thin soles that let the rider feel the stirrups. Boots could be as long as 16 inches, with a heel two inches in height. The large heel prevented the foot from sliding through the stirrup.

THE STETSON
In the 1860s, New Jersey hatmaker John B. Stetson designed a broad-brimmed hat to be worn on the open range. The Stetson became the most popular headgear in the West, and by 1900 the company was manufacturing more than two million hats a year.

JINGLE-JANGLE SPURS
Cowboys wore spurs on their heels to control their horses. To prevent cutting the horse, the cowboy filed down the spur's rowels until they were blunt. When he rode, his spurs jingled, a familiar sound that westerners termed "saddle music."

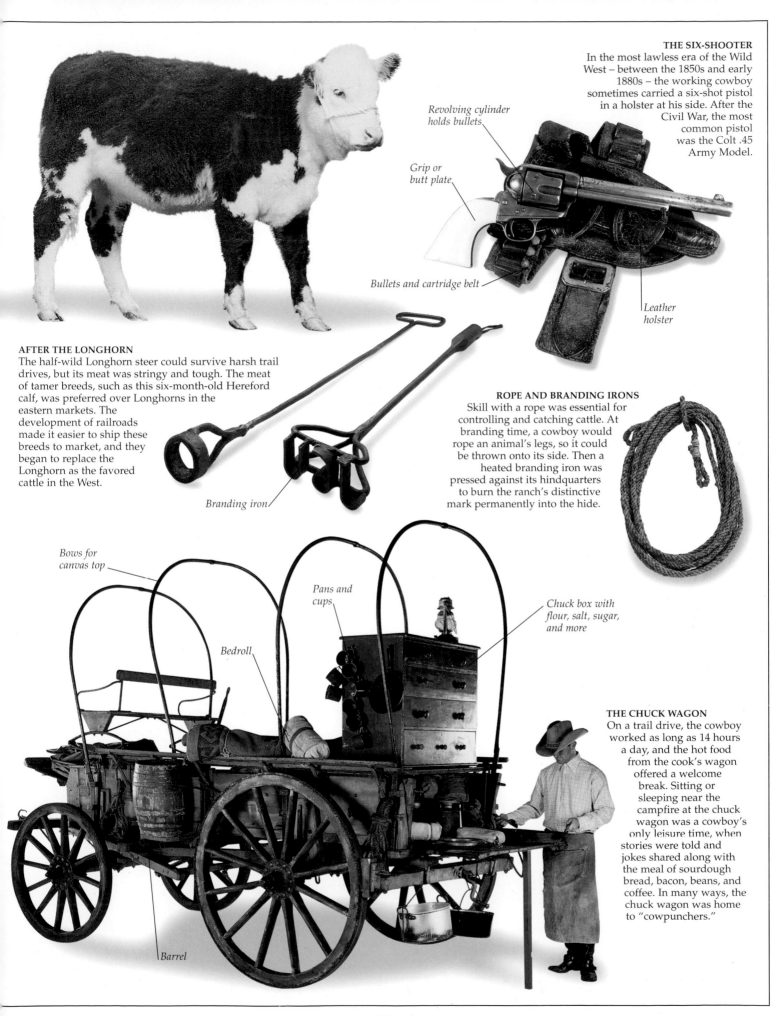

THE SIX-SHOOTER
In the most lawless era of the Wild West – between the 1850s and early 1880s – the working cowboy sometimes carried a six-shot pistol in a holster at his side. After the Civil War, the most common pistol was the Colt .45 Army Model.

Revolving cylinder holds bullets

Grip or butt plate

Bullets and cartridge belt

Leather holster

AFTER THE LONGHORN
The half-wild Longhorn steer could survive harsh trail drives, but its meat was stringy and tough. The meat of tamer breeds, such as this six-month-old Hereford calf, was preferred over Longhorns in the eastern markets. The development of railroads made it easier to ship these breeds to market, and they began to replace the Longhorn as the favored cattle in the West.

Branding iron

ROPE AND BRANDING IRONS
Skill with a rope was essential for controlling and catching cattle. At branding time, a cowboy would rope an animal's legs, so it could be thrown onto its side. Then a heated branding iron was pressed against its hindquarters to burn the ranch's distinctive mark permanently into the hide.

Bows for canvas top

Pans and cups

Bedroll

Chuck box with flour, salt, sugar, and more

THE CHUCK WAGON
On a trail drive, the cowboy worked as long as 14 hours a day, and the hot food from the cook's wagon offered a welcome break. Sitting or sleeping near the campfire at the chuck wagon was a cowboy's only leisure time, when stories were told and jokes shared along with the meal of sourdough bread, bacon, beans, and coffee. In many ways, the chuck wagon was home to "cowpunchers."

Barrel

Continued from previous page

Packing company symbol

Longhorn

The trail drive

Cowboys rounded up several thousand cattle for a trail drive – a three-month journey that could be as long as 1,200 miles. The herd was taken to new pasturelands or markets, or steered toward a cattle town for shipment by rail. After the Civil War, cowboys on these trail drives were a mixed breed. They included Mexicans, blacks, and Indians, and a large number were English and Scottish immigrants. When the drive was over, cowboys celebrated by enjoying the pleasures of a hotel and the food of a real restaurant. Often, they gambled away everything they had earned from the drive.

ON THE RANGE
Hardy Longhorn cattle, descended from Mexican breeds, ran freely over the range and were well adapted to the dry conditions of the Southwest and plains. Cowboys rounded up Longhorns each year until a herd was large enough to drive to a railhead, where they would be sold and shipped to market.

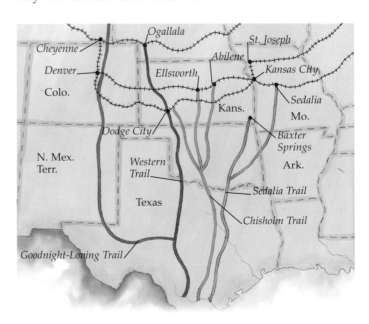

Major western cattle trails

Dangers on the trail

Drivers pushing herds along the trail faced many dangers, including storms that could cause cattle to panic and stampede. Occasionally, hostile Indians might strike, and wild animals could prey on young cattle. But the most dreaded danger was fording rivers that lay along the route. While a herd was being driven across the river, cattle and riders sometimes stumbled, were swept away by swift-running waters, and drowned.

RUSTLERS AND GUNPLAY
While it happened infrequently, cattle thieves could strike suddenly. Here, cowboys fire on Mexican rustlers trying to get away with cattle stolen in Texas.

STAMPEDE!
A herd was always ready to run if spooked, even on the main street of Dodge City, Kansas. Cowboys had to ride in front of the stampeding herd and fire pistols, crack whips, and whistle and shout to make the leaders turn aside. When the cattle were milling and confused, they stopped running.

The end of the range

At first, cattle grazed freely over the open range, but by the last part of the 19th century, thousands of miles of wire fences were being built. Both ranchers and sheepherders wanted to control the movement of their stock. In some regions, arguments over the right to fence in the range caused armed clashes, and opponents sometimes cut each other's wire. The growth of towns and large-scale agriculture further limited the open range throughout the West.

LOST ON THE TRAIL
The dried skulls of Longhorns littered the routes of cattle drives, testimony to harsh conditions and to the sudden death that stalked a herd along the way.

SHEEP ON THE RANGE
Cattlemen complained that sheep cropped grass too close for regrowth to occur and ruined water holes. At times, violence erupted between sheepherders and ranchers for control of the land.

IN THEIR OWN HANDS
Nebraskans demonstrate how some cowmen donned masks and took the law into their own hands, illegally cutting barbed wire fences to allow cattle to roam freely. These individuals carry fake wirecutters made of wood.

BARBED WIRE'S MANY SHAPES
Settlement of the West and the development of agriculture resulted in thousands of miles of barbed wire fences being erected to protect private property. Barbed wire fenced off the open range, angering cattlemen who had been used to letting their stock graze wherever there was grass.

Farming the West

GOVERNMENT HOMESTEADING POLICIES made western land cheap to buy, which encouraged rapid settlement. At first, most farms were worked by a single family, which cooperated with other families during the busy harvest time. The development of mechanized equipment for reaping, threshing, plowing, and planting soon made it possible to cultivate huge fields of crops such as corn and wheat. Windmills pumping groundwater for people, crops, and livestock were a familiar sight, since water was often in short supply. In 1867, many farmers united to establish the National Grange, a powerful political organization representing agriculture.

BUSTING SOD
Westerners who plowed the virgin soil were nicknamed "sodbusters." Here, a South Dakota homesteader works with a span of oxen yoked to his hand-held plow. Ground bones of buffalo were used to make a rich fertilizer.

MOWING FIELDS
This advertisement features the fast-moving Climax Mower, manufactured by the Corry Machine Company in Corry, Pennsylvania. The horse-drawn mower could cut from 8 to 15 acres of pastureland a day.

A FAMILY WINDMILL
The McCartys of Custer County, Nebraska, gather in front of their wooden windmill, which was essential for pumping water from depths of 200 feet or more. The "tail" of the mill kept it facing the direction of the wind, and also offered a space for advertising.

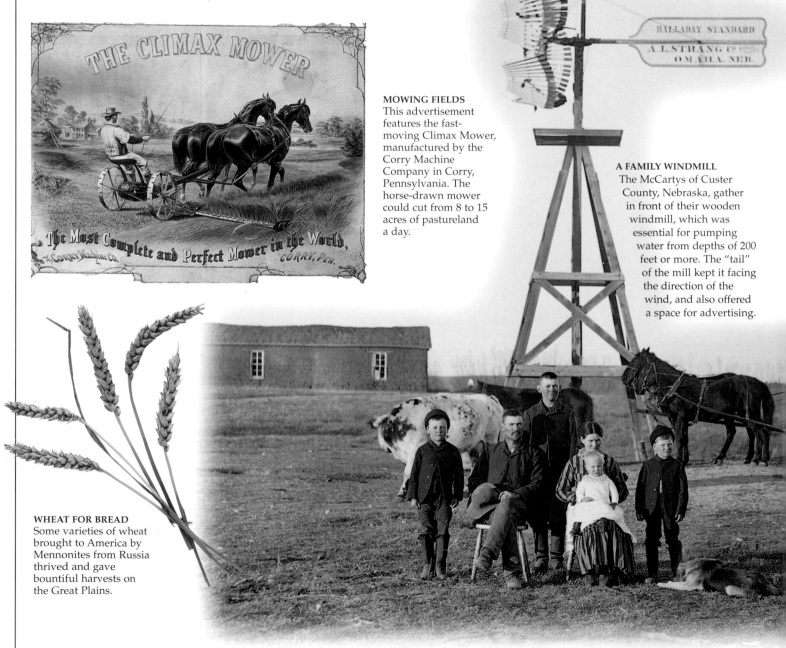

WHEAT FOR BREAD
Some varieties of wheat brought to America by Mennonites from Russia thrived and gave bountiful harvests on the Great Plains.

THE COMBINED HARVESTER
Mechanization of farming equipment made it possible for a single family to plant and reap enormous quantities of grain. This hard-working combine – meaning it combined many harvesting operations – cuts, threshes, and cleans the wheat as it is pulled by horses across fields near Walla Walla in Washington State.

Multi-purpose combine

33 horses harnessed together

GRAIN SHOVEL
Once grain was harvested and separated from the chaff, it had to be stored and kept dry. Shovels made from a single piece of wood were used to move grain into storage areas or into wagons for shipment to market.

CELEBRATING FARMING
A United States two-cent stamp issued in 1898 commemorated farming in America, an industry that was increasingly mechanized, with improved equipment that plowed, sowed, reaped, and gathered in the crops.

HAY HOOK
Muscle power and this wrought-iron hay hook lifted bales of hay into barns for storage until needed to feed stock during the winter.

"GIFT FOR THE GRANGERS"
This poster symbolized farmers throughout America, who united in the Patrons of Husbandry, commonly called Grangers. Politically powerful Grangers, with more than 800,000 members by the end of the 19th century, organized to guarantee fair treatment by state and national governments and to keep railroads from overcharging for shipping farm produce to market.

The West in legend

As the 19th century closed, the frontier West gave way to cities, livestock, large-scale agriculture, national parks, and oil wells. Outdoor enthusiasts and naturalists, such as Theodore Roosevelt, led successful efforts to preserve resources and protect open land, but the West was changing forever. As the "Old West" became more civilized, the romantic legend of the "Wild West" grew in popularity. The term "Wild West" sprang from touring shows that featured sharpshooting and trick riding, and reenactments of buffalo hunts, gunfights, and holdups. Fascination with the West was stimulated by the exciting "dime novels" that appealed to millions. Some of the first feature films ever made were "Westerns," which further exaggerated the image of the Old West as wild. America became enchanted by the frontier West – a time and place that would never return, but would not soon be forgotten.

The Wild West Show

Former scout of the prairie, William F. "Buffalo Bill" Cody, organized a Wild West show in 1883, and for 30 years it toured America and Europe. Sharpshooting Annie Oakley and famous cowboys were the stars of Buffalo Bill's Wild West. The most spectacular acts included a Pony Express relay race, a reenactment of "Custer's Last Fight," and an Indian attack on the Deadwood stagecoach. Even the great Sioux chief, Sitting Bull, joined the show and toured briefly during the 1885 season. It was Sitting Bull who gave Annie Oakley her well known nickname, "Little Sure Shot."

THE SHARPSHOOTING OAKLEY
Annie Oakley (Phoebe Ann Moses, 1860–1926) won her reputation by performing astonishing feats of marksmanship in Wild West shows. As part of her act, she would shoot a dime from between a partner's fingers. She once hit 943 glass balls out of 1,000 thrown into the air. Her life has been portrayed in fiction and comic books, television and movies, and in a Broadway musical called *Annie Get Your Gun*.

INDIANS AND COWBOYS, ROUGH RIDERS ALL
The thrills and action of Buffalo Bill's Wild West show leap from this advertising poster, which attracted young and old when the show passed through town. The "Rough Riders" included Arabs and Mexicans as well as Indians, cavalry, cowboys, and some beautiful ladies.

BUFFALO BILL (1846–1917)
Frontiersman William F. Cody did it all: Pony Express rider, Civil War combatant, scout for the army, and Indian fighter. As a hunter supplying buffalo meat for railroad builders, Cody earned the nickname "Buffalo Bill." Dime novels about his adventures won him fame, as did the Wild West shows he operated. To America and the world, Buffalo Bill became the best-known model of the legendary "Wild West" hero.

BEAR WRESTLING
The appeal of Western adventure sent audiences to traveling theatrical shows such as "The Great Train Robbery." This poster promises a wrestling match between a "cow-boy" and a grizzly.

A PRESIDENT'S COWBOY CHAPS
New Yorker Theodore Roosevelt loved his ranch in Dakota Territory. When he became President of the United States, he promoted national parks, protected forest lands, and preserved natural treasures such as the Grand Canyon, which was named a national monument in 1908.

Pockets

Leather fringes

REMEMBERING BLACK TROOPERS
This bronze statue depicts a mounted "Buffalo Soldier," as Indians called black cavalrymen. An enormous body of artwork has been inspired by the Old West's popular images, nostalgia, and lore.

THE NOBLE INDIAN
Elk Foot, a Taos Indian from New Mexico, posed for this 1909 portrait. Artist Eanger Irving Couse added a "coup stick," which Plains Indians carried, but the Taos did not. The blanket was from England, and the moccasins were from the studio. Yet, Elk Foot's fine features go beyond the staged aspect of the painting and present a striking, enduring image of the young Indian man.

DIME NOVEL THRILLS
Americans loved "dime novels" – so called because these books once cost ten cents – and adventure tales in magazines such as "Western Aces," from 1936.

A GHOSTLY RIDER
Like a phantom from a bygone era, this solitary horseman is silhouetted against the western horizon. He is a reenactor portraying an 1880s Oklahoma Territory lawman, who often rode alone while keeping the peace. Reenactors, in their turn, keep the memory of the Wild West alive and vivid for generations of Americans yet to come.

63

Did you know?

FASCINATING FACTS

The United States once almost got into a land war with Canada. In 1844, James K. Polk stirred up settlers during his presidential campaign by suggesting the United States would fight the British government over control of the Pacific Northwest. After Polk won the election, calmer heads prevailed and the Oregon Treaty of 1845 split the disputed territory at the 49th parallel between the United States and British Canada.

James K. Polk

Early settlers in the West had to make their own mattresses and other household goods. One side of a mattress was filled with feathers, preferably from geese, and the other side with a layer of straw or corn husks. The feather side would be on top in the winter and keep sleepers warm, and in summers, the mattress was turned over, because it was cooler to sleep on straw.

In 1869, Wyoming became the first territory or state to give women the right to vote.

Although ancient horses once lived in North America, they vanished between 8,000 and 10,000 years ago. They finally returned to North America with the Spanish in the 16th century. By the time of the Louisiana Purchase, thousands of horses again roamed the West.

In 1540, Spanish explorers became the first Europeans to see the Grand Canyon. Since they didn't find gold there, they quickly left. Then in 1824 soldiers from Missouri traveled down the Colorado River through the canyon. When they returned home, they told of what they had found. But the first real exploration of the Grand Canyon by white men didn't take place until 1869—329 years after the first Europeans visited it.

The outside walls of the Corn Palace in Mitchell, South Dakota, feature murals made of corn, wheat, oats, and other crops. Every year, the murals are recreated.

The *Shawnee Sun*, written in the Algonquian language and published in Kansas in 1835, was the first newspaper to be printed entirely in a Native American language.

On a trip up the Missouri River, John James Audubon described what he called "the curious notes" of the Western Meadowlark, whose song sounds like a flute. The bird is now the state bird of Kansas, Montana, Nebraska, North Dakota, Oregon, and Wyoming.

In 1830, the Indian Removal Act authorized the President to force the Choctaw, Chickasaw, Cherokee, Creek, and Seminole Indians out of the Southeast and onto lands set aside for them in what is now Oklahoma. In 1889, this land was officially opened to white settlers. Yet some homesteaders raced to claim land "sooner" than the official opening allowed. Today, Oklahoma is known as "the Sooner State" in tribute to those first white settlers.

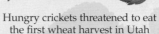

Hungry crickets threatened to eat the first wheat harvest in Utah

Although Utah is mostly desert and hundreds of miles from the nearest ocean, the state bird is the California gull. The first year Utah's Mormon settlers farmed by the Great Salt Lake, they faced a plague of crickets, which threatened their first crop of winter wheat just as it ripened. Nothing the settlers did got rid of the crickets, and without their wheat crop, the settlers faced famine. From out of nowhere came hordes of gulls, who ate up all the crickets—saving the crop and the Mormon settlement.

The oldest road in the United States is "El Camino Real," the Royal Highway. It follows an old Indian trail that runs between New Mexico and Mexico City. Early Spanish settlers to New Mexico used the road to journey north.

During prehistoric times, much of the Great Plains was under water. In 1995, scientists discovered the skeleton of a 23 foot (7 meter) marine lizard in North Dakota called a mosasaur. Today the creature's skull and bones are on display at the North Dakota Heritage Center in Bismarck, North Dakota.

"Stagecoach Mary" Fields was one of the toughest women on the frontier. Born a slave in 1832, she later worked as a hired hand for the Ursuline nuns in the Roman Catholic convent in Cascade, Montana. Over six feet tall, Mary carried a six-shooter and a rifle and was usually the winner in a fist fight. Because the local bishop disapproved of Mary, she eventually left the convent and began work delivering mail by stagecoach. No matter the weather, she never missed a day and delivered mail to even the most remote cabins. When she died in 1914, the entire town of Cascade mourned her.

In the winter of 1866–1867, Chinese workers who helped build the Transcontinental Railroad lived and worked in tunnels that were dug as deep as 40 feet (12 meters) under the snow.

To western pioneers, Nebraska's 325 foot (9 meter) tall Chimney Rock was an important landmark since it could be seen from miles away.

"Stagecoach Mary" Fields

QUESTIONS AND ANSWERS

Q Why is Phoenix, Arizona named for a mythological bird?

A Phoenix was founded in 1868 on the site of an ancient Hohokam Indian settlement built in about 300 C.E. Because of this ancient history, a settler suggested the name after an ancient myth about a bird that burned in its nest, only to arise from the ashes as an even more beautiful bird.

A mythological phoenix

Q If I'm lost in the desert, can I get water from a cactus?

A Because cacti store water for long periods of time in the dry desert, many people believe that it's possible to cut into a cactus to find drinking water. Unfortunately, this is not true. Cutting into a cactus would release a milky liquid. In some cacti, this liquid is poisonous, so drinking it would only make things worse for a thirsty hiker. Better to look for low-flying birds—a good sign that water is nearby.

Q How long are a longhorn's horns?

A Texas longhorn cattle indeed have very long horns, often measuring over 5-feet (1.5-meters) long, from tip to tip.

Q What battle killed the most Indians?

A The battle against diseases killed far more Indians than any military battle. With little or no immunity to microbes from Europe and elsewhere, Native people fell to diseases unintentionally introduced by whites. Sometimes whites used disease to intentionally harm American Indians. During the French and Indian War, British commander Sir Jeffrey Amherst is said to have distributed blankets infected with deadly small pox to infect and weaken Native populations.

Q Who was Joaquín Murieta?

A According to legend, Joaquín Murieta turned to crime after his family was attacked. In 1853, the California legislature hired Harry Love to bring Joaquín to justice. Love found a group of Mexican outlaws and killed their leader and one of his men. Love's men then cut off the head of one of the men and the hand of the other, packed them both in a whisky jar and sent the jar to the legislature with a demand for their reward. The head and hand were later displayed all around California. Whether this head belonged to the real Joaquín Murieta is not known.

Poster

Q Who was Jesse James?

A Jesse James was one of the most legendary figures of the Old West. He and his brother Frank robbed their first bank in 1866, and for the next 15 years, his gang robbed banks, stagecoaches, and trains throughout the United States. In 1881, Missouri's governor offered $10,000 to the person who could capture the James Brothers, dead or alive. One day, while Jesse was adjusting a portrait on the wall, Robert Ford, a member of his gang, shot him in the back and killed him.

Jesse James

Q Which colorful character was known as "the Emperor of the United States"?

A An Englishman named Joshua Norton arrived in San Francisco just after the start of the California Gold Rush. However, in 1853, he lost all his money. In time, Norton came to lose his sense of reality as well. He declared himself Norton I, Emperor of the United States, and began wearing a gold braided uniform and feathered hat. He printed his own money and used it at local restaurants, shops, and bars. San Franciscans were so fond of their "Emperor" that when he died in 1880, more than 10,000 of his fans attended his funeral to pay their respects.

Q Who was "Calamity Jane?"

A Although it's hard to separate the facts of her life from fiction, Martha "Calamity Jane" Cannary was one of the most famous women in the West. She wore men's clothes, swore, and drank. She was also an excellent shot and rider who won the respect of men like "Buffalo Bill" Cody and "Wild Bill" Hickok.

Timeline

THE SAGA OF THE AMERICAN WEST is one of the most dramatic in American history. The west was home to many thousands of Native American peoples at the time that the first Spanish explorers wandered the Great Plains and Southwest in the 1600s. When the United States purchased the vast Louisiana Territory from France in 1803, the lands were still largely unknown. Over the next century, as Americans moved west, some would battle Native peoples, others would seek their fortunes in gold and silver, and still others would help turn the vast Great Plains region into the world's richest farmland.

Cabeza de Vaca

1500s
Spanish explorers Coronado, Cabeza de Vaca, and Espejo, in separate expeditions starting in Mexico, explore the land north of the Rio Grande.

1754–1763
Great Britain defeats France in the French and Indian War.

1776
Fathers Escalante and Domínguez lead a group from Santa Fe seeking a route to California to link Spanish missions along the west coast.

1795
The United States and Spain sign the Treaty of San Lorenzo, which allows Americans to trade on the lower Mississippi River.

1804–1806
In 1804, Meriwether Lewis and William Clark and a team of explorers, scientists, and adventurers leave St. Louis, embarking on what will be an 8,000-mile journey to chart part of the new territory and the lands beyond.

A Spanish *santos*, or saint figure, dressed like the Franciscan priests who founded the California missions

1825
The Great Treaty held at Prairie du Chien, Wisconsin, sets the territorial boundary between the Sioux and Ojibwa Nations at the Red River, which is now the border between Minnesota and North Dakota.

1825
Congress declares much of what are now the states of Oklahoma and Kansas, land thought to be worthless for settlement, to be a permanent Indian frontier.

1830
The Indian Removal Act forces southeastern tribes into lands beyond the Mississippi.

Members of nine Indian tribes meet at Prairie du Chien to sign a treaty with the United States.

1832
During Black Hawk's War, the Sauk and Fox tribe, led by Chief Black Hawk, fight in vain against the U.S. Army, which is bent on forcing them out of Illinois and Wisconsin.

1834
Fur traders build Fort Laramie in Wyoming to protect and supply wagon trains heading west along the Oregon Trail.

headdress

peace medal

Wapello, a chief of the Sauk and Fox tribe

1834
The Department of Indian Affairs (the former Bureau of Indian Affairs) is given additional responsibilities by Congress to regulate trade with tribes and administer their western lands.

1835–1836
The Texas Revolution begins. On April 21, 1836, U.S. settlers defeat the Mexican army at the Battle of San Jacinto and form the Republic of Texas.

1843
The first major wagon train of more than 900 people and 1,000 head of livestock, arrives in Oregon Territory via the Oregon Trail.

1846–1848
The United States defeats Mexico in the Mexican-American War.

1847
The Mormons, members of the Church of Jesus Christ of Latter-Day Saints, settle at Utah's Great Salt Lake after traveling more than 1,100 miles (1,770 km) from Illinois.

1848
The California gold rush begins when gold is discovered at Sutter's Mill, California.

1854
Congress passes the Kansas-Nebraska Act, which opens the Kansas Territory to settlement by whites.

1859
Silver is discovered at the Comstock Lode in Nevada.

1860
The Pony Express begins to deliver mail between Missouri and California. The Pony Express lasts just over a year and is soon replaced by the transcontinental telegraph line.

1861
On October 24, telegraph wires in Salt Lake City are connected, linking the East and West.

1862
The Homestead Act opens up 160 acres of public western lands to settlement.

1867
The Chisholm Trail, used by cattle drivers, connects the large cattle ranches of South Texas to railheads in Kansas. The trail, which will operate until 1884, is one of the most famous cattle trails in the west.

1869
Chinese, Irish, German, Dutch, and other immigrants complete construction of the first transcontinental railroad.

1872
Congress creates Yellowstone Park in Wyoming to help conserve the nation's endangered national resources and as a recreational "pleasure-ground."

1874
Joseph Glidden and Isaac Ellwood build a factory in Dekalb, Illinois, to manufacture barbed wire where 10,000 pounds were largely produced by hand.

1876
James "Wild Bill" Hickok, hunting guide, gunslinger, and sometime lawman, dies after being shot while playing cards.

Ezra Meeker

Crazy Horse

1876
Sioux warriors under the command of Sitting Bull and Crazy Horse soundly defeat the 7th Cavalry, led by General George Armstrong Custer, at the Battle of Little Big Horn near Rosebud Creek in Montana.

1877
William "Billy the Kid" Bonney, age 17, kills his first victim.

1877
Chief Joseph of the Nez Perce leads 300 of his people on a 1,200-mile (1931-km) march to Canada to escape war with the U.S. Army. After much fighting and many casualties, Chief Joseph surrenders just 40 miles (64 km) south of his destination.

1881
Billy the Kid is shot and killed by New Mexico Sheriff Pat Garrett at age 21.

1881
Wyatt Earp and his brothers engage in a gun battle with outlaws at the OK Corral in Tombstone, Arizona.

1883
Former scout William "Buffalo Bill" Cody organizes the first "Wild West Show" and takes it on tour. Over the next 25 years, the Wild West Show travels across the United States and Europe.

1886
Geronimo, an Apache leader, surrenders to U.S. forces and he and his band of followers are taken into custody.

1887
The Dawes Act divides Indian lands into family holdings to break up tribal relationships and encourage self-sufficient farming—a practice that goes against their traditions and culture. Many of the Native Americans who agree to the plan receive land unsuitable for farming.

1906
Ezra Meeker takes the last wagon along the Oregon Trail.

Find out more

THERE ARE MANY WAYS to learn more about the Old West. You can retrace the path of the pioneers along the Oregon Trail or visit a southwestern ghost town. You can find personal accounts online about what life was like living in a sod house, or you can visit your local library for specialized books on the subject. Old western movies on TV are fun, though not always accurate, and action-packed documentaries tell the real history of the cowboys, gold miners, Indian chiefs, and more.

**BUFFALO BILL
HISTORICAL CENTER**
Visitors to the Buffalo Bill Historical Center in Cody, Wyoming can learn how "Buffalo Bill" Cody used his famous Wild West Show to spread the stories and legends of the Old West to an eager worldwide audience—even before television or radios existed. Visitors to the Historical Center can also enjoy traditional drumming and dancing at the annual Plains Museum Powwows adjacent to the museum, test their sharpshooting skills at the Buffalo Bill Invitational Shootout, and view one of the largest collections of western art in the world.

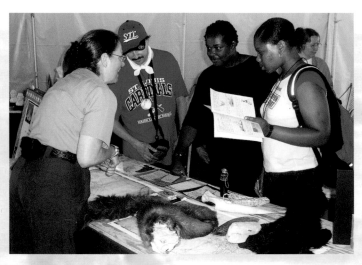

GATEWAY TO THE WEST
Visitors to the Museum of Westward Expansion in St. Louis, Missouri, listen as a park ranger explains how fur trappers worked their trade. Visitors can also try numerous organized activities that challenge them to make the decisions that American Indians, cowboys, and pioneers on the Oregon Trail would have made. Save time for visiting the Odyssey Theatre for a larger-than-life glimpse of Lewis and Clark's journey produced by National Geographic.

USEFUL WEB SITES

- A fascinating look at the American West from the pages of *Harper's Weekly*, the illustrated 19th century newspaper:
  http://thewest.harpweek.com

- Another great site on the history and development of the American West:
  www.americanwest.com/

- More than 30,000 photographs of the Old West from the Denver Public Library:
  lcweb2.loc.gov/ammem/award97/codhtml/hawphome.html

- Companion site to the PBS series, *The West*:
  www.pbs.org/weta/thewest/

- Online version of *Wild West* Magazine:
  www.historynet.com/we/

Tarp covering

TRAVEL THE OREGON TRAIL
The Oregon Trail stretched 2,170 miles (3,492 km) from Independence, Missouri, to the Columbia River region of Oregon. Of all the famous western trails, it was in use for the longest period of time. Even today, many local tour guides take visitors on horseback or covered wagon along the route so they can experience the adventure.

SOD HOUSES

At the Sod House Museum in Aline, Oklahoma, you can visit one of the few original sod houses still standing on the Great Plains. In Gothenburg, Nebraska, you'll find sod house recreations—as well as amazing displays of barbed-wire art—including a life-size buffalo and a horse with Native American rider.

Infantryman's fatigue cap

THE ARMY LIFE

Find out what life was like for soldiers in the U.S. Army at forts across the West from costumed military reenactors. These "soldiers" are at Fort Larned, once an important garrison in Larned, Kansas.

THE REAL-DEAL WILD WEST

Many famous Western towns, like Dodge City, Kansas; Deadwood, South Dakota; Virginia City, Nevada; and Cripple Creek, Colorado attract thousands of visitors looking to learn about life and times in the 19th century American West. These visitors to Tombstone, Arizona, are preparing to set off on a stagecoach tour of the town.

Places to Visit

THE ALAMO
SAN ANTONIO, TEXAS
When you visit San Antonio's famous landmark, be sure to watch the short film, produced by the History Channel, about the most famous event in the Texan Revolution.

MUSEUM OF THE AMERICAN WEST
LOS ANGELES, CALIFORNIA
Founded by Gene Autry, the famous "Singing Cowboy" of Hollywood westerns, the museum features a collection of items celebrating Autry's career. Also included are exhibits on cowboy life, California history, law enforcement, and more.

MUSEUM OF THE MOUNTAIN MAN
PINEDALE, WYOMING
This museum tells the story of the Rocky Mountain fur trade era. Each year, it also hosts Green River Rendezvous Days, a re-enactment of an historic fur-trapper rendezvous.

SMITHSONIAN NATIONAL MUSEUM
OF AMERICAN HISTORY, BEHRING CENTER
WASHINGTON, D.C.
The Museum offers three floors of exhibitions that explore the rich diversity of American history, including many artifacts from the Old West.

SMITHSONIAN NATIONAL MUSEUM
OF THE AMERICAN INDIAN
WASHINGTON, D.C.
The newest museum operated by the Smithsonian Institution features exhibits on the important ideas and experiences in native life and history.

NEZ PERCE NATIONAL HISTORIC PARK
SPALDING, IDAHO
This giant park includes 38 sites in Idaho, Oregon, Washington, and Montana that tell the history of the Nez Perce nation.

VIRGINIA CITY HISTORIC DISTRICT
VIRGINIA CITY, NEVADA
Tour the famous Comstock Lode silver mine that made Virginia City one of the wildest boomtowns in the West.

Glossary

ADOBE Brick made of clay, straw, and water, formed in a mold and dried in the sun

APOTHECARY A person such as a pharmacist who prepares and sells medicines and drugs

BARBED WIRE Twisted strands of wire with barbs at regular intervals to prevent cattle and other livestock from escaping

BRAND A mark burned on the hide of an animal with a hot iron to show ownership of that animal

BRIGHAM YOUNG Leader of the Mormons following the death of Joseph Smith, the religion's founder

CANOE A light, slender boat with pointed ends propelled by paddles

CARBINE A light shoulder rifle with a short barrel, often used by the cavalry

CATTLE RUSTLER A cattle thief. Some cowboys would steal another man's cows by branding them with their own brand; the infamous Clanton Gang of Arizona would steal cows from one man and sell them to another.

CLAIM JUMPER A person who illegally took possession of another person's claim to land or a mine

COLT .45 A make of revolver invented and manufactured by Samuel L. Colt; the most popular of Colt's many different caliber guns

CONQUISTADOR The Spanish word for "conqueror," used to refer to the 16th century Spanish explorers of South, Central, and North America

COWHAND A man hired to care for cattle, also known as a cowboy, "cowpoke," or "cowpuncher"

DRAFT ANIMAL An animal such as a mule or ox that is used for pulling heavy loads or transporting goods

DRY GOODS Ready-to-wear clothing, fabric, and other textiles, as opposed to jewelry, groceries, hardware, or wet goods

EMIGRANT A person who leaves one country to settle in another; used to refer to settlers from the eastern United States who settled in the west

GENERAL STORE A country store that does not specialize in one kind of product but carries groceries, clothing, tools, and almost any other kind of products needed by customers

HACIENDA The Spanish word for the ranch or estate of a large landowner; also the word for the house on the ranch

HOMESTEADER A farmer who took up land under homesteading laws, such as the Homestead Act of 1862; used by cowboys to refer to any kind of farmer

Sluice

IMMIGRANT A person who enters a new country to settle there after having left his or her homeland, such as the Chinese, Irish, Russians, Swedes, and Germans who made new lives for themselves by settling in the west

INTERPRETER A person who translates from one spoken language to another

Variety of goods offered

General store on the Navajo reservation in Arizona

Lariat

LARIAT A throwing rope with a running noose used for catching animals; from the Spanish word *la reata*

LATTER DAY SAINTS The formal name for the members of the Church of Jesus Christ of Latter-Day Saints, or Mormons, who first settled near Utah's Great Salt Lake in the late 1840s

Prospectors

SODBUSTER Another nickname given by cowboys to farmers; early farmers who settled on the Great Plains built their homes out of sod, the grass-covered top section of the soil that is held together by matted roots.

SOMBRERO A broad-brimmed straw or felt hat worn in Mexico or the Southwest

TRIBUTARY A stream or river that flows into a larger stream or river. The Missouri, Red, Arkansas, and Ohio Rivers are all tributaries of the Mississippi River, which was one of the most important means of transportation before the railroads.

WAGON TRAIN A group of wagons carrying settlers from the east to Oregon, Utah, California, or elsewhere in the west

WESTERN SADDLES Saddles used in the west for riding horses; different from "Eastern" or "European" saddles in that they were originally designed for work rather than show

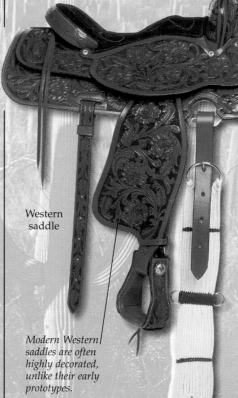

Western saddle

Modern Western saddles are often highly decorated, unlike their early prototypes.

LEVI'S Today, a common term for blue jeans, the rugged pants first designed for miners by Levi Strauss and Co. of San Francisco

MARSHAL A federal lawman who was responsible for carrying out orders of the court

MELTING POT A place made up of many different immigrant groups, races, and cultures

MISSION A church built by Catholic priests, especially in Spanish-held parts of North America, such as California, Texas, and New Mexico, built to help convert local Indians to Christianity

Moccasins

MOCCASINS Soft leather slippers worn by American Indians

NOMADIC Moving from place to place, surviving by hunting and gathering for food rather than by permanent farming

OPEN RANGE An unfenced area in which animals are free to wander and graze. Before barbed wire fences, most of the Great Plains were open range.

PRAIRIE Flat or rolling grasslands, as found on the Great Plains

PROSPECTOR One who explores an area for gold, silver, or other natural deposits

QUILLED Made with a length of reed, cane, or shaft of feather, around which yarn is woven

RENEGADE An outlaw; from the Spanish word *renegado*

RESERVATION A piece of land set aside by the U.S. government for American Indian tribes. The majority of reservations were located west of the Mississippi River. Today, the largest is the Navajo reservation in northern Arizona and New Mexico.

RITUAL A special ceremony or practice that is held for a specific purpose, such as part of a religious observance

SERAPE A blanket commonly worn by Mexicans as a shawl, often folded narrowly and neatly over one shoulder as decoration

SIX-SHOOTER A revolver that contains six bullet chambers; sometimes called a "six-gun" or a "shooting iron"

Six-shooter

SLUICE A man-made channel for flowing water using a valve or gate to control the speed or amount of water's flow; used by miners to run water over lighter soil, leaving only gold behind

Bullet chamber

Index

Acknowledgments

The author and publisher offer their grateful thanks to: Ellen Nanney and Robyn Bissette of the Product Development and Licensing Department of the Smithsonian Institution; Richard E. Ahlborn, Paul F. Johnston, Jennifer L. Jones, Larry N. Jones, Ramunas Kondratas, David H. Shayt, Alonzo N. Smith, Lonn Taylor, Roger White, and Bill Withuhn of The National Museum of American History, Behring Center; Nancy A. Pope of the National Postal Museum; Gregory Marx, owner of Frontier Americana.

Photography Credits:
t = top; b = bottom; l = left; r = right; c = center
Atlanta History Center: 54bl. Bill Ballenberg: 22cl. Michael Brannin: 18br. Buffalo Bill Historical Center, Cody, WY: 50tr. California State Library: 20br, 26cr, 27cl, 39tr. © California State Parks, 2001: 53cr. © David Cain: 12tr, 16cl, 25br, 58br. Daughters of the Republic of Texas: 23br. Denver Public Library, Western History Collection: 29b. DeSoto NWR, U.S. Fish & Wildlife Service: 21tc, 34cl, 34c, 35cl. Dover Publications: 51tc, 52tr, 59tl, 59tr. El Rancho de las Golondrinas: 23cl, 23cbr.

Everglades National Park: 17br. The Fred Hultstrand History in Pictures Collection, Institute for Regional Studies, NDSU, Fargo, ND: 32tl, 35b, 43c, 43br. Golden Spike National Historic Site: 40b. © Judy Hedding: 7br. The High Desert Museum, Bend, Oregon: 31cr, 33bl, 34bc, 34bl, 42c. Independence National Historical Park: 12cl, 12c. Jefferson National Expansion Memorial/National Park Service: 30cr, 31tl, 31cl. The Kansas State Historical Society, Topeka, Kansas: 19br, 53bl. © Farron Kempton, GhostRiders of Tulsa (rider: Tim Ridgeway): 63br. Kentucky Historical Society: 15tlc. Library of Congress: 11t, 12bl, 13cr, 14b, 15tl, 15tr, 15blc, 15brc, 15bl, 16cr, 17tl, 17cr, 18–19t, 18cl, 18cr, 19tr, 20bl, 22–23c, 23tl, 24tr, 24bl, 24br, 25tl, 25tr, 25c, 25cr, 27cr, 27bl, 27br, 28tr, 28c, 29tl, 31b, 32tl, 32br, 36tr, 37bl, 39cr, 41tr, 41cr, 42t, 43tr, 43bl, 44–45cr, 46–47tr, 46bl, 46br, 47ctr, 47cbr, 49tl, 49tr, 50br, 51tl, 52b, 53tl, 54tr 55tl, 56tl, 58tl, 58bl, 60tr, 60cl, 61br, 62cl, 63tl. Gregory Marx, Frontier Americana: 13br, 18bl, 19bl, 19bc, 21cl, 21c, 27tr, 30tr, 31tr, 38tl, 38tr, 38br, 41tl, 44tl, 44cbl, 50cbl, 51cb, 52cr, 54bc, 57tr. Minnesota Historical Society: 55tr, 55b.

Montana Historical Society: 35tr, 45bl. MPI Archives: 7tl, 22bl, 24ct, 33br, 34br, 47br, 61cl, 61c. Museum of Church History and Art: 29c, 31c. Museum of the Mountain Man: 19cbl. National Anthropological Archive: 47tr, 48bl, 49tc. National Archives: 11b, 21tr, 39tl, 49cr, 49b, 50cr, 61t. National Museum of American History: 12cr, 15br, 20t, 21 br, 24cl, 25cl, 23tr, 30tr, 32bl, 37br, 39br, 41bcl, 41br, 45br, 48cl, 48ctr, 51tr, 54cl, 54br, 56bl, 56br, 59br, 62bl, 63tc, 63tr, 63cr. National Museum of Natural History: 9tr, 10c, 13cl, 13c, 27tl, 27c, 46tl, 47bl. National Museum of the American Indian: 8bl, 9tl, 10tr, 11cl, 15trc, 17bl, 48cbr, 48br. National Park Service: 12bc, 12br, 14tl, 22tr, 28bl, 28br, 34–35th, 38bl, 44tr, 44br, 45tl, 45tr, 48c. National Portrait Gallery: 62tr. National Postal Museum: 13tl, 37tl, 37cl, 41bcr, 61cr. National Zoological Park: 6cr, 6b, 7cr. Nebraska Dept. of Economic Development: 6tr. Nebraska State Historical Society: 33t, 43tl, 59bl, 60–61b. North Carolina Museum of History, Raleigh: 23bl. Presbyterian Historical Society: 54cr. Reprinted with the permission of Pinkertons, Inc: 51ct, 51bl. Smithsonian American Art Museum: 8bl, 8br, 9cl, 9br, 10bl,

10br, 13tr, 26bl, 63bl. St. Joseph Museum, St. Joseph, Missouri: 36b, 37tr. State Historical Society of North Dakota: 21tl. Union Pacific Railroad Museum: 40t, 41ctl, 42b. Used by permission, Utah State Historical Society, all rights reserved: 29tr. West Point Museum: 48tr. Collection of Mark Winter: 23ctr. Woolaroc Museum, Bartlesville, Oklahoma: 16b. Wyoming Tourism Office: 6tr.

Jacket Credits: *Front:* Tc: Buffalo Bill Historical Center; Tcr: Gregory Marx for www.FrontierAmericana.com; B: © CORBIS. *Back:* Tr: MPI Pictures; C: Library of Congress; Ccr: National Museum of the American Indian; Cr: National Museum of American History;
Br: West Point Museum; Cl: Neil Lukas © Dorling Kindersley, courtesy of the Wells Fargo History Museum, San Francisco.

NB: All Web sites listed in this book were active at the time of publication. DK Publishing and the Smithsonian Institution are not responsible for their content.